Weddings
& Courtships
Italy

Love and Romance
The Italian Way

Lisa Shea

This is the fully updated front-to-back revised 2015 version of the book I first wrote in 2002.

Contents

Weddings
& Courtships
Italy

Introduction

*"O Romeo, Romeo! wherefore art thou
Romeo?
Deny thy father
and refuse thy name;
Or, if thou wilt not, be
but sworn my love,
And I'll no longer be a Capulet."*
—Shakespeare, Romeo and Juliet

I taly and Rome have perhaps done more to shape love and romance ideals than any other culture in the world. The Roman gods and goddesses of the past give us the cherubic Cupid; Venus, the goddess of love; and Mars, god of war. Anthony and Cleopatra's love affair still resonates today. The star crossed lovers of Shakespeare's Romeo and Juliet captivate modern audiences. The love, passion, loyalty and honor that goes with the ideals of Italian love are legendary.

The Italians loved art and beauty, and celebrated both in abundance. Italian stories tell of romance found and lost. Italian artists created paintings telling a thousand tales of couples that overcome difficulties to be together. Numerous stories and movies are set in Italy, as its rich, lush landscape immediately brings to mind the passion and tumult of love.

Against this raw passion, Italy is also very religious and very traditional. A family is a sacred bond, one to respect and honor. Young women are seen for their potential as mothers, and are treated with concern and encouragement. Any appreciation offered by a man should be done very respectfully, for to disrespect a daughter is to incur the wrath of the father and brothers.

A married woman is also appreciated for her charm and grace, and given much respect. A family sticks together – a couple would not speak against each other in public, and would defend each other should the need arise. Signs of tenderness and love are expected, and even long-married couples can be seen kissing and holding hands in the streets of Rome.

Read on to bring Italian romance into your life.

Salute—Health!

A History of Italian Love

*Within my Lady's eyes abideth Love,
Hence where she looks all things
must needs grow kind, And when
she passeth all men glance behind,
And those she greeteth such
fond raptures prove That
from each downcast face
the color fades And every
fault repentance doth
inspire:
Before her flee presumptuousness and ire...*
—Dante Alighieri 1265-1321

I t would seem that the entire culture of Italy is based on tales of love lost, love found, of romance, and family. The Roman gods were always falling in and out of love, and drawing mortals into their schemes. Love could move mountains and launch a thousand ships. The stories and tales of Italy often involved thepower of love and the importance of family.

Cupid

While not a real person, Cupid was the God of Love to ancient Romans, and many Italians believed in his powers. Even in the modern world, references to Cupid and his bow and arrows of love are found everywhere on Valentine's Day.

Cupid was not initially the cherubic, happy little angel that we think of today. In his original incarnation, he was a very mischievous, sometimes dark god of love and desire who enjoyed matching 'odd couples' and seeing how they worked out.

Cupid eventually fell under his own spell of odd matches. He fell in love with Psyche, a mortal. In the Greek language, Psyche means "butterfly" and also means "soul". In many ways, what Psyche goes through is symbolic of the path of each woman's soul in life.

Cupid had actually been sent by his mother, Venus, to punish Psyche for her beauty. Instead, he was captivated by her. He arranged to have her brought to his mountain home to live with him, but he hid his identity from her, only visiting her at night. Their time together was so tender and full of gentle talk that Psyche fell in love with Cupid, without ever seeing him.

Psyche's jealous sisters were angered by her wealth and love, and convinced Psyche that her lover must be a monster to so hide himself. The sisters persuaded her to sneak up on him after he left her one evening, armed with a knife. He awoke and saw her there, and said sadly, "I inflict no other punishment on you than to leave you forever. Love cannot dwell with suspicion."

Psyche realized how foolish she'd been, and decided the only way to be with Cupid again was to go talk to Venus and ask for her blessing. Venus was delighted at having Psyche kneeling down before her, and set forth many tasks for Psyche to perform to prove her worthiness. Each task was more than Psyche thought she could manage, but in each case a God stepped in to assist her. Finally Psyche and Cupid were allowed to be married. They were very happy together, and had a child, named Pleasure.

Bring cupid into your life by drawing hearts with arrows in them on the steamy morning bathroom mirrors, or by signing your letters and notes with the symbol!

Venus

One of the most important mythological figures in Italy was Venus. Venus was the goddess of love and passion. Young men and women would pray to her in the hopes of finding a caring lover, or to catch the eye of a person they'd already fallen for. She was both the goddess of chastity in younger woman, and full sexual desire and love in older women.

Venus actually traces her history to the Greek goddess, Aphrodite, who was also a beautiful goddess of love. Many of Aphrodite's stories were simply translated to the Roman world and applied to Venus. Venus had many love affairs and relationships, both with other gods and with mortals. She could be extremely gracious to those who prayed to her and hoped for love and happiness.

The city of Venice was named after this goddess, and each year they celebrate in her honor. Julius Caesar and Emperor Augustus both worshipped her and claimed to be descended from her.

Venus' symbols were the rose, myrtle, and doves. All three symbolized love and passion to the Italians.

Send roses to your love, or keep a myrtle sachet in your bedroom to bring you the passion of Venus!

Saint Valentine

Saint Valentine was a Roman who was killed for his faith on February 14, 269 A.D. He had refused to worship pagan gods, and some stories say he was a priest who would marry young couples in secret who loved each other but who did not have parental permission. In 496, his 'saint day' was established. He is associated with love because he fell in love with the daughter of his jailer, and would pass notes to her. His final note, before he was executed, read 'from your Valentine'.

In Italy, with its romantic and religious roots, St. Valentine's Day became the traditional day to be engaged. Young Romans would spend this day gathered together in gardens to listen to romantic poetry and music.

As with many holidays, the celebration of St. Valentine's Day became a mixture of the new Christian rites as well as the older pagan rites of that same time of year. St. Valentine's Day happened to fall on the Roman festival of Lupercalia. This festival was held each February to protect the villages from wolves, who would at this point be starving and cold and begin to make their village raids.

During the festival of Lupercalia, young men would playfully whip women with stripes of animal hide, chasing them around town. It was felt that this festival made the women who were 'whipped' more fertile. The young men would sometimes draw the names of girls from a jar, to choose their partner for the day for any singing and dancing.

February 14 is a great day to celebrate with your own valentine, but don't forget the other days of the year! Send each other notes, full of poetry!

Anthony and Cleopatra

Even after 2,000 years, Cleopatra is still a well-known name whose adventures have inspired stories, plays, and movies. Cleopatra was the daughter of an Egyptian king who took the throne at age 17. She was beautiful, intelligent, and cunning. She spoke 9 languages and was excellent at math, geography, history, and many other subjects.

According to the traditions of those days, Cleopatra married her brother, the 11 year old Ptolemy XIII. She wanted more for herself, though – love, for one, and a secure homeland. The Romans came calling when she was 21 years old. Seeing her opportunity, she seduced Julius Caesar in a novel fashion. She had her servants wrap her in a carpet and bring her to Caesar as a present. Caesar was 54 years old at the time. Cleopatra went with Caesar back to Rome and bore him a son, which they named Caesarian.

Only four years later, the Italian people grew tired of Caesar's adoration of this foreign woman. For that and other reasons, Caesar was assassinated and Marc Anthony and the emperor Octavian took power.

During the next three years, Cleopatra seduced Marc Anthony, and he returned with her to Egypt. Although Marc Anthony legally married Octavian's sister to keep the peace, he was still in love with Cleopatra and spent most of his time with her. She would scatter roses at his feet and take rosewater baths with him. Finally he divorced Octavian's sister and married Cleopatra in 32 BC.

Octavian was furious at this, and declared war on the couple. After many battles, his forces finally defeated those of Cleopatra and Marc Anthony. Facing capture and torture by 30BC, the two lovers committed suicide. While this is a sad ending for the pair, they lived their lives with great love, passion, and respect for one another's intellect and knowledge. Live your own life with the same fervor!

Romeo and Juliet

This fictional couple from Venice is perhaps one of the best known romantic couples today. In the late 1500s, Shakespeare constructed the tale of two warring families in a way which touches the heart of all that read the story or watch it performed. This play was based on Masuccio Salernitano's story of the two lovers, penned in 1476. A series of poems were then written about this story by both French and Italian authors. In 1562, Arthur Brooke wrote a long poem entitled "A Tragical History of Romeus and Juliet," bringing the tale to the current populace. Shakespeare read this and decided to adapt it into a play. The story therefore had been known to audiences for over 100 years, but Shakespeare's lyrical language made it a classic for the ages.

The story of Romeo and Juliet portrays both the power of young love and the importance of family in Italy. While the two are madly in love with each other at the young end of marriageable age in Italy (12 for girls, 14 for boys), the fighting between the families created a barrier between Romeo and Juliet. The two lovers realized it would be a serious step to disobey their families and be together, but their love for one another overcame their concerns.

Even with this love, their religious upbringing holds them to a true course. Romeo's respect for his Juliet is absolute, and they go to great lengths to find a priest to properly marry them before they run off together. Their time together after the marriage is more than either could ever have hoped for. Their tragic end, both committing suicide when they believe the other is dead, causes their families to repent and to mend the rift. The two lovers are together forever in death, and the families have found a peace.

The play has been put on thousands of time and adapted into many film versions, including the Zeffirelli version of 1968, the DiCaprio version of 1996, and *West Side Story*.

While the ending is sad, the thought of a love being powerful enough to stand against all odds is a potent one. If your love is facing obstacles, stand fast against them! No matter how difficult your own obstacles might seem, remember that there are others who faced even more serious difficulties, and overcame them.

Renzo and Lucia

In the early 1800s, Alessandro Manzoni created his work "I Promessi Sposi" or "The Betrothed". The tale is set in the 1600s in Milan, Italy – a time of great warfare and violence, of cruel rulers and the peasants who try to survive as best they can. During this time, a plague is spreading through Milan, and adds to the tension.

In the middle of all of this chaos, the story tells of the blossoming love of a young peasant couple, Renzo and Lucia. Unfortunately for the pair, Lucia's beauty has attracted the eye of the local ruler, Don Rodrigo. The lovers attempt to marry, but Don Rodrigo disrupts their plans and forces them apart. The two overcome many obstacles before they finally find their way back to each other to be together.

At last, a traditional Italian story with a truly happy ending! Renzo and Lucia were neither rich nor royal. They were simple peasants who loved each other dearly. Against a powerful foe, they triumphed and stayed true to each other in the end. Find that same commitment and valor in your own love life!

Courting and Dating the Italian Way

"Can it be that love fills my heart and
brain?
If love, dear
God, what is its
quality? If it is
good, why does
it torture me?
If evil, why this
sweetness in my
pain? If I burn
gladly, why do I
complain?"
—Petrarch (1304-1374)

Ah, Italy. The lush landscapes and famous love stories lead one to believe that courting in Italy was a passionate, love-filled affair. However, the process was far more one of a familial joining than a love match sought by two individuals. Most marriages until recent years were arranged, and were put together by the fathers who wished to raise their family's rank or gain more land. The "proper" young woman would be kept inside during most of her childhood, safe from harm. She would often only see her intended husband through her window, talking to him from the safety and propriety of the second floor. Even in the poorer communities, the young girls were protected as much as possible, so they would not be stolen away by bandits or have their chastity compromised.

Only in current years, when women are allowed more freedom and independence, could they go out and date a boy of their choosing. Even so, the dates tend to be with groups of friends, so that the two are not alone. Still, progress is being made!

An Italian woman has been considered the epitome of beauty, grace, style and gentleness. This was not because she sprang out of the sea perfectly formed, as did the goddess of love, Venus. Rather, it is because Italian girls were trained from birth to focus on those arts which would enhance their attractiveness. An Italian woman had to make herself of value to her family, so that the family would not become poor by supplying a dowry to get her a husband. She had to be skilled in cooking, cleaning, and needlework, and educated enough to be a good teacher to her children. In addition to these things, she did her best to be as lovely as possible, to attract the chosen mate.

An Italian woman was therefore well educated in how to apply cosmetics, and would often spend two or more hours preparing her face before being seen. She would have many types of cosmetics and brushes and know how to use them in different situations. She would also understand the different uses of hair styles, combs and ribbons to give different impressions to her suitor—that of intelligence, capability, innocence, sweetness—whatever was necessary. Italian seamstresses were world renowned for their skill in enhancing and improving any body shape imaginable, so she would be clothed in the most appropriate outfit to match her physical gifts.

While Italian women of the earlier years were instructed to be dutiful and obedient to their husbands, times have changed. An Italian woman is no longer the servant of her husband. In current times, Italian women are famous for their fiery tempers and their strong wills. With the women still putting so much time and effort into their presentation, they want to get a response worthy of that effort from their suitor. After so many hours of preparation, she insists on being appreciated. Now it is up to the man to prove that he is pleased by the effort. He is expected to wine and dine her, to treat her with the utmost respect, and to show his undying affection.

It is said that one of the skills of an Italian male is to be able to make every woman in a room feel appreciated and admired by him, without any woman feeling disrespected in any way. Quite a challenge in any culture, but a skill to be cultivated, indeed!

A History of Dating in Italy

"But now I am return'd
and that war-thoughts
Have left their places
vacant, in their rooms
Come thronging soft and
delicate desires,
All prompting me how
fair young Hero is,
Saying, I liked her ere I
went to wars."
—Shakespeare, *Much Ado about Nothing*

Italy is a land of family and friends. When people go out in the evenings, they go out in groups of friends, to listen to music, talk for hours, have fun and enjoy themselves. In times past, a woman's reputation was extremely important to her and to her family. If a young man wished to take her out alone, usually an older woman was sent along as a chaperone, to ensure that things stayed proper. Tradition tells that, as the evening got darker, the chaperone would keep a lighted candle between the couple, to be able to see exactly how close they got to one another. In fact, this has resulted in the Italian term "regerre il moccolo", which literally describes the candle in the middle.

Most single Italians were looking forward to a life involving a home, a profession, and a family with lots of children. The future husband had this firmly in mind when he sought his spouse, with the constant instruction of his own family. This bride would be expected to cook large meals for the family, to keep up the house work and the farm work, and tend the vegetable and herb gardens. A lazy wife would quickly bring shame on the husband and his entire family. So, to the Italian man, a hard working woman was a better catch than a pretty one who spent all of her time on herself.

In the same manner, Italian women wanted to marry a man that could provide well for their own needs and that of their family and children. If her siblings ran into trouble, her husband would be expected to help them out. The woman would expect to have proper ingredients for her meals, to have fine cookware on which to serve them, and especially to have the proper clothing and jewelry with which to adorn herself. So, while a handsome husband might be a nice thing to hope for, a more practical desire was for a husband who was stable and who could provide properly for her and her family.

The Colors of Italy

In the days of the Roman Empire, the colors of gold and red stood for the glory of Rome. When the Roman Empire collapsed, Italy dissolved into numerous provinces, each with its own ruler and flag. For example, Messina's flag is red and yellow, and Palermo's features a colorful coat of arms on a burgundy background. Genova's flag has a red and white cross, Rome's city flag is red and yellow, and Verona's is white and red.

If you know what area of Italy your family traces its roots to, you may want to learn more about its flag, and use its colors in your decorating.

It was only in 1848 that the 'Kingdom of Italy' decided on the green, white, and red flag, featuring a red and white cross (the Royal Arms) in its center. In 1946 Italy moved to a flag just with the three colored bars, representing its change to a republic.

The current Italian flag is comprised of red, white and green, and many Italian restaurants use red and white checkered tablecloths. Both bring to mind Italian culture for us in modern times.

Italian Family Colors

With family being so important to the Italians, the family colors were often far more important than the colors of the area where you lived. A family determined where you lived, who you married, and even had a lasting impact on your adult life. While kingdoms came and went, the family survived it all.

Here are some of the more common Italian surnames, with the colors associated with them. If your name is not listed here, you may want to research your family's colors. You could introduce them into your environment, and share in the pride of your ancestors.

Andretti: silver and red
Amato: white and red
Amorello: red and silver, on blue and gold
Bernardi: gold and black
Bianco: blue and silver
Blanco: blue and silver
Bonanno: gold and black
Campanella: red
Corona: blue and gold
Corvo: gold and black
Costa: red, silver and black
Delgado: red and green
D'Agostino: silver and red
DiMaggio: blue and black
Esposito: silver, red and green
Gallo: red and gold
Genovese: blue, red, silver and gold
Giglia: blue and yellow
Giovanni: blue and gold
Leonardi: red and gold
Marino: silver and black
Medina: gold and red
Moreno: gold and black
Morena: gold and black
Nardi: blue, silver and gold
Navarro: blue and red

Palminteri: green and yellow
Pesce: blue and silver
Pini: red and green
Pucci: silver and black
Romero: red and gold
Rossi: silver and red
Sabatino: gold, blue and red
Sacco: red and silver
Stefano: silver, green and gold
Testa: red and gold
Trevino: gold and blue

Italian Flowers and their Meanings

Italians were exceedingly practical people when it came to flowers and gardens. They adored fountains and made sure that fountains were located in town centers and in gardens, where the water could be both beautiful and useful. They created elegant shapes out of shrubs and trees, and included elegant sculptures for added visual appeal.

Italians would rarely disturb this order with flowers just for the sake of having flowers. Valuable garden space would not be wasted on pretty, but useless plants. Instead, gardens would hold vegetables and herbs, to please the eye, the nose, the appetite, and the palate. Common vegetables in gardens would be radishes, cucumbers, red onions, and artichokes.

Bouquets carried by girls and by brides were most often filled with herbs. Myrtle was associated with Venus, the goddess of love. Each herb had a different meaning to the Romans:

sage: wisdom, respect oregano: joy

basil: romance dill: fertility

rosemary: remembrance

garlic: protection from evil spirits

But, in their gardens, the Italians have always made room for roses. The Italian culture loved roses. Gardens would hold bouquet roses, climbing roses, rose bushes, roses of every shape and size. Cleopatra scattered rose petals at Marc Anthony's feet, and Nero had them fall from the ceiling during his dinners.

Each type of rose soon took on its own particular meaning, and Italians were very knowledgeable about which types of roses sent specific messages.

red rose: passionate love white rose: innocence, purity

red and white roses together: unity, marriage

pink rose: appreciation, friendship

yellow rose: joy

rosebuds: youth, innocence

Rosewater has been used since ancient Roman times for the cleansing of hands, and as an elegant way to bathe. In the 1500's, women commonly used rosewater for washing their hands and bathing, to keep their skin young and fresh smelling. Try this yourself to delight your skin and senses!

Homes often had window boxes, and a walk down an Italian street would draw your eye to these brightly filled mini-gardens. Common balcony flowers include geraniums, cyclamens, dahlia, zinnia, petunia, sunflower, and violet. Of these, violets were often given to dates, as a sign of faithfulness and loyalty.

Related to flowers is the elegant glasswork called millefiore, or 'thousand flowers'. This glass style originates in Murano and involves thousands of little glass flower designs to be connected together to form an overall pattern for a vase, cups, plates, or other glassware. A beautiful vase of millefiore is often given along with flowers, to show that the flowers you give are eternal, like your love.

Italian Music and Song

Italians have always loved music. Whether it was a stringed lute, a shepherd's flute, a rich guitar or the more complex workings of opera or orchestra, the Italians loved it. They took pleasure in folk songs at the end of a day of work, in rich chorals during their day of prayer and worship, and full orchestral creations for special events. It is no accident that many of the world's great operas were written in Italian!

Read on to learn more about the wide variety of music which has been produced in Italy.

Italian Folk Songs

Italians are immersed in folk music from the day they are born. It is common for an Italian household to have a guitar or pipe in a corner, and for families to sing and play together in their free time. Evenings spent with family and friends are often highlighted by singing and music.

For lovers, music was an integral way to convey your feelings to your partner. A young woman would sing down to her beloved, and the man would serenade her from beneath her window.

One of the more popular songs in traditional circles is "O Sole Mio", which talks of the joy of being with a person you love.

Che bella cosa e'na jurnata 'e sole,	What a beauty is a day of sunshine,
n'aria serena doppo na tempesta!	a clear blue sky when the storm is over!
Pe' ll'aria fresca pare gia' na festa	The fresh air is like a festival Che bella cosa
e'na jurnata 'e sole.	What a beauty is a day of sunshine
Ma n'atu sole	No other sun
cchiu' bello oi ne'.	is more beautiful than this
'O sole mio	My own sun
sta 'nfronte a te!	from your dear face!
'O sole, 'o sole mio	My sun, my own sun
sta 'nfronte a te!	is in your face!
sta 'nfronte a te!	is in your face!
Lùcene 'e llastre d''a fenesta toia;	How sparkling are your window's glasses
'na lavannara canta e se ne vanta	The cleaning lady sings
and boasts	
e pe' tramente torce, spanne e canta	She wrings, hangs out, and sings
lùcene 'e llastre d'a fenesta toia.	How sparkling are your window's glasses
Ma n'atu sole	No other sun
cchiu' bello oi ne'.	is more beautiful than this
'O sole mio	My own sun
sta 'nfronte a te!	from your dear face!
'O sole, 'o sole mio	My sun, my own sun
sta 'nfronte a te!	is in your face!
sta 'nfronte a te!	is in your face!
Quanno fa notte e 'o sole se ne scenne,	When evening approaches and the sun is
setting	
me vene quase 'na malincunia	a sense of sorrow comes
over me	
sotto 'a fenesta toia restarria	I remain here under
your window	
quanno fa notte e 'o sole se ne scenne.	When evening approaches and the sun is
setting	
Ma n'atu sole	No other sun
cchiu' bello oi ne'.	is more beautiful than this
'O sole mio	My own sun
sta 'nfronte a te!	from your dear face!
'O sole, 'o sole mio	My sun, my own sun
sta 'nfronte a te!	is in your face!
sta 'nfronte a te!	is in your face!

Antonio Vivaldi

Born in Venice in 1678, Antonio was pushed into priesthood although he did not show much interest in it. He spent much of his adult life as a music teacher at the Ospedale della Pieta, in essence a place where the unwanted female children of rich Italian nobles were sent to be educated.

Vivaldi wrote operas and concerti, as well as vocal works for his students. He is perhaps best known for his "Four Seasons" concerto, in which each section of the composition relates to one of the seasons. He had a strong impact on musicians of his day, and brought the use of strings into fashion.

Vivaldi traveled extensively and was linked with the singer, Anna Giro, with whom he stayed until his death. He died in 1741 from bronchitis.

Vivaldi wrote sonnets to go with each season in his Four Seasons work. Here are his sonnets which accompany the spring movements:

Movement 1

Here comes the Spring, and festively The birds salute her with a merry song

And fountains, to the whispering Zephyrs With sweet murmurings flow all the while. Advancing o'er the heavens is a black canopy With lightning and thunder to announce her. Then, when they go silent, the little birds Return anew to their cheerful song.

Movement 2

And later in the lovely flowering fields To murmurings of fronds and leaves The goat herd sleeps,

His faithful dog beside.

Movement 3

To the rustic bagpipe's festive sound Nymphs and shepherds dance 'Neath Heaven's canopy,

And Spring appears so brilliantly.

Italian Opera

Italy is famous for its development of the musical style known as opera. The first opera was performed in the year 1600, at the wedding of Henry IV of France and Marie de Medici. They were married in Florence, Italy at the Pitti Palace. The opera was called Eurydice and told the story of Orpheus and Euridice. This was a classic Greek myth which tells of the lovers Orpheus and Euridice. On their wedding day, Euridice is bitten by a poisonous snake. Heartbroken, Orpheus descended into Hell to plead for her return. His song is so tender and loving that Persephone, Queen of the Underworld, convinces her husband, Hades, to release Euridice.

At the time, the performance style was of long recitations of stories with musical accompaniments, and the actors would speak loudly to be clearly heard.

By 1637 the first opera house had opened in Venice. As more and more operas were written, the use of different vocal parts and richer musical styles became popular. Opera was wildly popular and new operas were greeted with great enthusiasm. As the years went on, the allure of opera spread around the globe.

Gioacchino Rossini was one of the most famous opera composers in the early 1800s. His works include the Barber of Seville, Otello, and William Tell. In the late 1800s, Verdi took on the mantle of one of Italy's greatest opera composers, creating the operas Aida and Falstaff, as well as his own version of Otello.

Italian Love Poetry

Poetry has a long history in Italy. There were many great poets during the days of the Roman Empire, and their audience stretched over much of the empire. Italian children were raised on poetry, and as they began courting, poetry was very much a part of the wooing.

Learn more about the poets of Italy, from the Roman Empire to the Renaissance and beyond!

Ovid

Publius Ovidius Naso was born in 43 BC in the Sulmona region of Italy. He went to law school and was taught by some of the finest instructors in Italy. He was on the path for an incredibly successful career in politics, but he decided to become a poet instead.

Ovid's love poetry was very controversial, and he was exiled for writing works such as Ars Amatoria (The Art of Love). This humorous piece taught men and women how to seduce and enjoy each other.

Ovid's work "Metamorphoses" is still taught in schools today, and his love poetry still touches the heart.

In one section of Ars Amatoria, the poem reads:

If there is anyone in this city who does not know the art of loving Let him read this poem and, having read it, love like a professional. By art are swift ships propelled by sail and by oar,

By art are light chariots driven. Love, too, must be ruled by art. Automedon was good with chariots and supple reins,

Tiphys was the helmsman on the Haemonian ship. Venus has set me up as a master over Love,

I shall be called the Tiphys and Automedon of Love. He is wild and one who will often struggle against me, but he is still a boy, a soft age ready to be corrected.

Ovid goes over all the details for both men and women. Following is a great passage where he warns the man to look good – but not to spend too much time beautifying himself. Feel free to take his advice to heart!

Don't delight in curling your hair with tongs, don't smooth your legs with sharp pumice stone.

Leave that to those who celebrate Cybele the Mother, howling wildly in the Phrygian manner.

Male beauty's better for neglect: Theseus carried off Ariadne, without a single pin in his hair. Phaedra loved Hippolytus: he was unsophisticated: Adonis was dear to the goddess, and fit for the woods. Neatness pleases, a body tanned from exercise:

a well fitting and spotless toga's good:

no stiff shoe-thongs, your buckles free of rust, no sloppy feet for you, swimming in loose hide: don't mar your neat hair with an evil haircut: let an expert hand trim your head and beard.

And no long nails, and make sure they're dirt-free: and no hairs please, sprouting from your nostrils. No bad breath exhaled from unwholesome mouth: don't offend the nose like a herdsman or his flock. Leave the rest for impudent women to do,

or whoever's the sort of man who needs a man.

Sextus Propertius

Sextus Propertius wrote The Love Elegies during the classical days of the Roman Empire. These tales told about his love affairs, and his passion and heartbreak.

In this section, Sextus is arguing with his friend, who is trying to get Sextus away from his current mistress Cynthia. Sextus praises his mistress, and warns his friend that by trying to drive the two apart, the friend is risking the wrath of the woman.

Why do you urge me to alter, and leave my mistress, Bassus, praising so many lovely girls to me? Why not allow me to spend the rest of my life in increasingly familiar slavery? You can praise Antiope's beauty, the daughter of Nycteus, and Hermione of Sparta, all those the ages of beauty saw: Cynthia denies them a name. Still less would she be slighted, or thought less, by severe critics, if she were compared with inferior forms. Her beauty is the least part of what inflames me: there are greater things I take joy in dying for, Bassus: Nature's complexion, and the grace of many an art, and pleasures it is best to speak of under the silent sheets.

The more you try to weaken our love, the more both disappoint with acknowledged loyalty. You will not escape with impunity: the furious girl will know of it, and will be an enemy to you with no unquiet voice. Cynthia will no longer look for you after this, nor entrust me to you. She will remember such crimes, and angrily denounce you amongst all the other girls: alas, you will be loved on never a threshold. She will slight no altar of her tears, no stone, wherever it may be, and however sacred.

No loss hurts Cynthia so deeply as when the god is absent, love snatched away from her: above all mine. Let her always be so, I pray, and let me never discover cause in her for lament.

Dante

One of the most famous Italian poets is Dante Alighieri (1265- 1321). This youth of the middle ages came from a good family, and was raised in an atmosphere of love and poetry.

At age 9, Dante met Beatrice and fell in love with her. Even though each went into arranged marriages with other people, Dante's love poetry was always directed towards Beatrice. She was the ideal woman to him, and many say that perhaps it was the distance they kept, and the fact that he only admired her from afar, that allowed his ideals of her perfection to remain so unblemished.

Dante began writing his poetry at age 18. Here is one of Dante's works about his beloved Beatrice.

La Vita Nuova

In that book which is My memory . . .

On the first page

That is the chapter when I first met you

Appear the words . . . Here begins a new life

Petrarca

Another famous medieval Italian poet was Francesco Petrarca, who wrote his famous collection of poetry "Rime in Vita e Morta di Madonna Laura" sometime in the mid-1300's. He wrote these poems for a young woman, Laura, that he saw in church but never became involved with. He wrote her 365 poems, all showing his adoration for her.

This translation is done by the About.Com Italian Guide, Michael San Filippo, who has kindly agreed to share his translations with us. He has quite a wealth of information on Francesco Petrarca and the Italian language in general on his site. Be sure to visit Michael's website to learn more about Petrarca and his sonnets!

Era il giorno ch'al sol si scoloraro per la pietà del suo factore i rai,

quando ì fui preso, et non me ne guardai, chè i bè vostr'occhi, donna, mi legaro.

Tempo non mi parea da far riparo contra colpi d'Amor: però m'andai secur, senza sospetto; onde i miei guai nel commune dolor s'incominciaro.

Trovommi Amor del tutto disarmato et aperta la via per gli occhi al core, che di lagrime son fatti uscio et varco:

Però al mio parer non li fu honore ferir me de saetta in quello stato,

a voi armata non mostrar pur l'arco.

Translation:

It was the day the sun's ray had turned pale with pity for the suffering of his Maker when I was caught, and I put up no fight, my lady, for your lovely eyes had bound me. It seemed no time to be on guard against Love's blows; therefore, I went my way secure and fearless— so, all my misfortunes began in midst of universal woe.

Love found me all disarmed and found the way was clear to reach my heart down through the eyes which have become the halls and doors of tears.

It seems to me it did him little honor to wound me with his arrow in my state and to you, armed, not show his bow at all.

•••

Quando fra l'altre donne ad ora ad ora Amor vien nel bel viso di costei, quanto ciascuna è men bella di lei tanto cresce 'l desio che m'innamora. I' benedico il loco e 'l tempo et l'ora che sí alto miraron gli occhi mei, et dico: Anima, assai ringratiar dêi che fosti a tanto honor degnata allora. Da lei ti vèn l'amoroso pensero, che mentre 'l segui al sommo ben t'invia, pocho prezando quel ch'ogni huom desia; da lei vien l'animosa leggiadria ch'al ciel ti scorge per destro sentero, sí ch'i' vo già de la speranza altero.

Translation:

When Love within her lovely face appears now and again among the other ladies, as much as each is less lovely than she the more my wish I love within me grows.

I bless the place, the time and hour of the day that my eyes aimed their sights at such a height, and say: 'My soul, you must be very grateful that you were found worthy of such great honor.

From her to you comes loving thought that leads, as long as you pursue, to highest good, esteeming little what all men desire; there comes from her all joyous honesty that leads you by the straight path up to Heaven— already I fly high upon my hope.

Giuseppe Gioacchino Belli

Starting in the early 1800s, Giuseppe Gioacchino Belli crafted his work. His family was extremely poor, and he finally found a job doing low-level government work in Rome. He wrote over 2,000 sonnets about the life and world he saw around him. Many were very humorous and appealed to the general population.

These two translations were done by Andrea Pollett, who has many great poems from Belli on his website. Andrea has kindly allowed us to share a translation here.

Here is a poem told from the point of view of a servant, who is observing a couple trying to choose a husband for their daughter.

La Scerta

Sta accusì. La padrona cor padrone, Volenno marità la padroncina

Je portonno davanti una matina, Pe sceje, du' bravissime perzone.

Un de li dua aveva una ventina

D'anni, e du' spalle peggio de Sanzone; E l'antro lo diceveno un riccone

Ma aveva un po' la testa cennerina.

Subbito er giuvinotto de quer paro Se fece avanti a dì: "Sora Lucia, Chi volete de noi? parlate chiaro".

"Pe dilla, me piacete voi e lui", Rispose la zitella; "e ppijerìa

Er cicio vostro e li quadrini sui".

Translation:

<u>The Choice</u>

This is how it went. My master and mistress, Wishing to have their daughter married

One morning brought in front of her Two very respectable persons to choose.

One of the two was about twenty

Years old, and had shoulders wider than Samson's; While the other one was known as a rich man

But had a few grey hair.

Immediately the young man of the couple Started saying: "Miss Lucy,

Who of us do you want? speak frankly".

"Really, I like both of you",

Answered the unmarried girl; "and I would take Your tool and his money".

Note that 'tool' in this poem is a reference to the young man's sexual organ.

Here is another tale told by a widower whose wife has passed away. After mourning for a while, the widower is now in love with his sister in law, and she with him. The poem shows how their love and persistence overcame the laws that tried to keep them apart.

<u>La Dispenza Der Madrimonio</u>

Quella stradaccia me la sò lograta: Ma quanti passi me ce fussi fatto Nun c'era da ottené pe gnisun patto De potemme sposà co mi' cuggnata.

Io c'ero diventato mezzo matto, Perché, dico, ch'edè sta baggianata
C'una sorella l'ho d'avé assaggiata E l'antra no! nun è l'istesso piatto?

Finarmente una sera l'abbataccio Me disse: "Fijo se ce stata coppola,
Pròvelo, e la licenza te la faccio".

"Benissimo Eccellenza", io jarisposi:

Poi curzi a casa, e, pe nu dì una stroppola, M'incoppolai Presseda, e
ssemo sposi.

Translation:

The Wedding License

I've worn out that damned street: But in spite of all this walking

There was no way to obtain the permission To marry my sister-in-law.

It was driving me crazy Because, I say, what a nonsense

That I already had a taste of one sister, But not the other! Isn't it just
the same?

Finally one evening the damned abbot

Told me: "My dear, if there has been copulation, Prove it, and I'll
give you the license".

"Very well, Excellency", I answered: Then I rushed home and, not to
tell a lie,

I had sex with Praxedes, and we got married.

You can see from these poems that while the Italians had a strong desire to handle romantic arrangements properly and to follow the rules, they also had a keen sense of humor about the process!

Italian Words and Phrases

Anyone who has seen the movie A Fish Called Wanda understands how a few phrases in a foreign language can go a long way. Jamie Lee Curtis, playing a woman named Wanda, became passionately aroused whenever she heard the rolling words of Italian on her lover's tongue. Add some spice to your own life by finding new nicknames for each other in Italian!

beautiful: bello
darling: tesoro
dear: caro
heart: cuore
husband: marito
kind: gentile
loyalty: lealta
love: amore
maybe: forse
no: no
sweet: dolce
sweetheart: inamorato
tenderness: tenerezza
wedding ceremony: sposalizio
wife: moglie
yes: si
I love you: ti amo
Will you marry me? volontà lo sposate

Cooking Up an Italian Romance

Friends are like pasta.
If they're not warm, they're not good.
—Italian Proverb

Italian food and romance are inextricably bound to one another. The image of a romantic Italian meal is classic. It begins with a pair of starry eyed lovers holding hands at a candlelit Italian restaurant. The food is piled high, a wine bottle stands open, and a trio of musicians serenade them. Even cartoons show this scene, such as in the classic Disney film Lady and the Tramp!

Here are some great Italian recipes to create your own romantic evening! Be sure to light the candles, grab a bottle of Chianti, and turn down the lights. Put on some lovely Italian music and you'll be set!

Pears and Cheese

Italians often enjoy cheese and fruit together. Many simple meals are made up of these two items, and perhaps a piece of bread. It's a great way to begin a meal or to tide you over until dinner. This dish is a perfect companion to prosecco—a sweet Italian sparkling wine.

6 pears

½ pound pecorino cheese

Black pepper

Peel the pears and cut them into 1" cubes. Dice up the cheese and mix it in. Let the mixture stand for about 10 minutes to blend properly, then top with freshly ground black pepper.

This is a perfect appetizer before the main meal is served.

Bruschetta–Italian Garlic Bread

Garlic bread has been a favorite appetizer in Italy since the days of ancient Rome. It can be found at just about every Italian restaurant today.

8 slices Italian bread
2 large cloves of garlic 1 tsp salt
2 tsp fresh ground black pepper
3 Tbsp extra virgin olive oil
2 tomatoes
8 basil leaves
parmigiano or reggiano cheese (grated)

Put the bread on a foil-lined cookie sheet and toast it lightly in an oven at 350°F (177°C). Cut the cloves of garlic in half and rub the bread with garlic while the bread is still hot. Season with salt and pepper, then soak each slice in oil.

Slice up the tomatoes. Put two slices of tomato on each piece of bread. Top each piece of bread with a basil leaf. Sprinkle with parmigiano and/or reggiano cheese and serve immediately.

If you're really a garlic lover, you can even chop the garlic up into small pieces and sprinkle these on top at the end, just before serving.

Italian Bay Scallops

Italy is surrounded by water, and it's no surprise that many Italian dishes involve seafood. This dish is delightful with a pinot grigio.

1 lg onion
1 green pepper 1 clove garlic 1/4 cup olive oil
16 oz can whole Italian tomatoes 1 tsp black pepper
1 Tbsp butter
1 lb bay scallops
1 Tbsp lemon juice
1/2 cup dry white wine
1 cup Italian bread crumbs

Dice the onion and the green pepper. Chop the garlic. Blend all three together in a pan with the olive oil and sauté for 3-5 minutes. Cut the tomatoes into small cubes. Add the tomatoes and the pepper. Simmer for 15 minutes.

Now sauté the scallops in butter until lightly brown. Add in the lemon juice and wine, and simmer for 7 minutes. Add the scallop mixture into the onion blend.

Pour all into a greased 9x9 baking pan, and sprinkle bread crumbs over the top. Bake at 375°F (190°C) for 30 minutes.

Lasagna

Lasagna is a dish with a long history. Ancient Romans named this dish after the 'lasanon' pot they cooked it in. Pre-Christian tombs show carvings of pasta tools, indicating the importance of pasta in this culture.

Lasagna:
9 lasagna noodles, cooked and drained 2 cups ricotta cheese
1 egg, beaten
1/2 cup parsley, chopped
1/2 cup parmesan cheese, grated 2 cups mozzarella cheese, grated
3 cups meat sauce (see ingredients below)

Meat sauce:
1 lb ground beef
onion, large, chopped 3 cloves garlic, minced 1 bay leaf
tsp basil, dried
1 1/2 tsp oregano, dried 2 Tbsp olive oil
3/4 cup red wine
3 28 oz cans crushed tomatoes
tsp salt
1/2 tsp pepper

To make the sauce, heat the oil in a large pan. When hot, add the beef and sauté for 5 minutes until lightly brown. Add the onion, garlic, basil, and oregano and continue to cook until the meat is well browned. Add the bay leaf, tomatoes, red wine, salt, and pepper and bring to a boil. Reduce the heat to medium low and simmer for 45 minutes. Taste and add salt and pepper if needed.

To make the lasagna, in a bowl, mix the ricotta cheese, beaten egg, parsley, and parmesan cheese together until well blended. In the bottom of a 9 x 13 inch baking dish, spread out 1/2 cup of sauce then place three lasagna noodles on top. If they do not overlap it is fine, they will spread out during baking.

Now spread 1/2 of the ricotta mixture on top of the noodles and sprinkle a little mozzarella over it. Now spread about 3/4 cup meat sauce on top of that and place the next layer of noodles on top and repeat the ricotta and mozzarella layers. You should end with the last layer of noodles on top. Spread the rest of the sauce on the noodles and top with the remaining mozzarella cheese.

Bake uncovered at 375 °F for about 45 minutes until the cheese is melted and bubbly. When done, let the lasagna sit for 10 minutes before serving.

Lasagna goes well with a fresh garden salad, Italian bread, and a Chianti.

Tiramisu

This traditional dessert doesn't require any cooking, and is quite delicious! Savor it by candlelight with a shared cup of coffee. It seems that every meal in Italy ends with coffee and a long conversation.

1/2 cups coffee, sweetened
1/4 cup sherry
50 lady fingers
4 egg yolks
3 tablespoons superfine sugar
1 pound mascarpone cheese
1 tablespoon baking cocoa

Mix together the coffee and about 2 tablespoons of sherry. Coat all of the lady fingers in this blend by dipping them into the mix.

In another bowl, mix together the egg yolks and sugar. Add in the cheese slowly. Mix in the rest of the sherry.

Put about half of the lady fingers along the bottom of an ungreased 10" cake pan. Now add a layer of half of the mascarpone cheese. Sprinkle on half of the cocoa powder. Now make another layer of coffee-dipped lady fingers, add another layer of mascarpone, and sprinkle on another layer of cocoa powder.

Refrigerate for 3-4 hours before serving.

Italian Wines

Wine in itself is an excellent thing.
—Pope Pius XII

Italy is the number one producer of wine in the world, and most Italians feel strongly that wine should be drunk with every meal. The traditional toast in Italy is 'Salute!'—to your health! With all of the recent discoveries about wine and health, the Italians knew what they were talking about!

Some of the more famous wines from Italy are Chianti, Soave, Amarone, Asti Spumanti, and Marsala. Learn more about these wines, and raise a toast to your own health!

Quick Food-Wine Pairing:

Chianti: spaghetti and meatballs, lasagna, veal parmesan Soave: vegetables, light cheese

Amarone: ripe game, rich dishes, heavy cheese Asti Spumanti: strawberries, peaches, fruits Prosecco: appetizers like fruits and light cheese

Marsala: nuts, spicy cheeses, sipping in the evening

Chianti

In the past, Chianti was the basket-bottle wine, served on a red checked tablecloth, holding a romantic candle. In a modern reworking, Chianti now often comes in a standard glass bottle, presenting a more elegant image. If you are a traditionalist, some brands still do use the basket to protect the bottle from harm.

Chianti comes from the Chianti region of Tuscany, Italy. Only wines from this region can properly be called Chianti, although some other areas are using the name on their labels.

Chianti is a red wine, strong and bold. It typically accompanies well-seasoned foods, like veal parmagiana, spaghetti and meatballs, and lasagna. Current marketing of the Chianti name includes a "Black Rooster" emblem—wineries in the Chianti Classico region have started using this rooster to build regional recognition for their wines.

Chianti is the perfect wine to go with that rich, romantic meal you've made. Think of the scene in Lady and the Tramp with the two dogs at the Italian restaurant, being serenaded, sharing a plate of spaghetti and meatballs? That was the perfect, romantic, Chianti meal!

Soave

Soave comes from Verona, land of Romeo and Juliet. The word "Soave" means gentle. Tradition has it that the famous thirteenth-century poet, Dante, who enjoyed spending time in Verona, gave Soave the name because of its mildness. He, and many others of his time, praised its qualities as a wine for light foods. Perhaps its refreshing qualities cooled him after a long day in summer heat.

There are three styles of Soave:

soave—the dry, still white wine

spumanti—a sparkling version

recioto—a sweeter version

Soave is a straw yellow, shading sometimes to green. It's known to be delicate and light, with perhaps a hint of almonds. Think of perfumes and gentle flowers. It carries a gentle acidity, and has a slightly bitter finish. No wonder this is a drink that lovers long for.

Soave is best as a before-dinner drink—with hors d'oeuvres or soups. It can also go with light dishes, like simple vegetables, rice, pasta, and the like. It's best served around 48°F. And of course, it is best shared with a book of poetry and someone you love.

Amarone

Amarone della Valpolicella, or Amarone for short, is created in the Venitian region of Italy. Originally, there was only one legal region, or DOC, for the Valpolicella name. These wines are made with Corvina Veronese, Rondinella and Molinara grapes. Two sub- groups emerged, though—recioto, which is a sweet dessert wine, and amarone, which is a dry red wine with great body.

Both of these wines are made with grapes that have been dried on racks, bringing out their flavors. In 1991, these two were granted their own DOCs. The land area encompassed by these three DOCs is the same, but the types of wine are quite different.

Amarone is the fourth biggest seller in Italy, behind Chianti, Asti, and Soave. This fine wine has flavors of licorice, tobacco, and fig, and goes well with game and ripe cheese. Hannibal Lechter of Silence of the Lambs fame, of course, had his amarone with fava beans. It's only in the movies that they converted his fondness to the more common Chianti.

While some styles of Amarone can be very bitter (that's where the name comes from), new styles are more fruity.

Amarone can be drunk young, while still a ruby purple, but it also ages magnificently to a dark garnet for thirty years or more. A typical drinking age is 10 years. Amarone should be served around 60°F.

Asti Spumanti

A non-Champagne-sparkling-wine, Asti Spumanti comes from the Turin region of Italy, in the upper northwest area. Asti is very popular with wine drinkers because it's very sweet and easy to drink. It's also much less expensive than its Champagne cousins.

Asti Spumanti is made from Muscat Canelli grapes. Asti is the town that actually supplies the grapes, while "Spuma" means "foam". It is a light yellow color, and is sweeter than typical French Champagne.

Asti Spumanti goes very well with sweet desserts—a dish of strawberries, or a sweet peach pie. It is the perfect ending to a meal for lovers, to toast to the sweetness of their love.

Prosecco

This sweet version of sparkling wine comes from the northeast part of Italy, and is made primarily from the prosecco grape. This is a perfect wine for a pre-dinner starter. Prosecco has a light, flowery aroma and goes well with fruits and cheese. It should be served at around 40°F.

Marsala

Marsala and Much Ado About Nothing both hail from the southern Italian island of Sicily. The movie version, starting Kenneth Branagh and Emma Thompson, is a beautiful statement of Italian love and emotion. There are thundering horses, witty retorts, gorgeous Italian countryside and a relatively happy ending. What other wine could you drink but a fine, rich Marsala, born in the hills of Sicily?

Much Ado About Nothing is based in Messina, to the north of Sicily, where one love is based on outer beauty, while the other rests with inner emotions. Marsala is a town to the west, where fortifying wines with brandy allowed the wines to travel to Britain, where they were soon in high demand. The home of Shakespeare supported this island's wine production.

Deceptive appearances, which helped Don John bring down fair Hero, also helped delicious Marsala during prohibition. In the US during this time, typical Marsala bottles gave the wine an appearance of medicine. People found that getting Marsala was less risky than other types of wine. It became extremely popular and has retained its popularity over the years. It has a rich, raisiny flavor and is often used in cooking meat dishes.

When the two happy couples had their wedding feast, undoubtedly Marsala was served between the first and second courses. For modern day couples, it can also be served, chilled, with Parmesan (stravecchio), Gorgonzola, Roquefort and other spicy cheeses.

Ideas for Italian-Style Dates

Do you have a sweetheart that you want to spend an Italian-style evening with? Here are some great ideas to get you started.

A Rich Italian Meal

The Italian social life revolves around food! Don't settle for pizza at the local pizza place! Pizza is actually a Greek dish that was popularized in the US. Instead, find a romantic Italian restaurant that serves traditional favorites along with a bottle of Chianti. Enjoy the romantic music and ambiance, and get into an Italian frame of mind.

A Classic Italian Movie

There is a list of great Italian movies later in this book, and many of them are love stories. Grab a copy of Cleopatra or Gladiator for a movie that you'll both love.

A Night at the Opera

Italy is the birthplace of opera, and many of the world's greatest operas were written by Italians. Go to a romantic opera of love and romance, and revel in the experience and the music.

Finding a Mate

"It is my lady, oh, it is my love!

Oh, that she knew she were!"

—Romeo, speaking about Juliet

Italy was a very religious land, and marriage was a sacred vow made before by God. An Italian match was a joining of two families, and was overseen by the fathers of each family. Often matchmakers would be used to find the most suitable combination of rank, wealth, and land for a given youth.

There were also love matches, where the two individuals would disregard any advice given by the families, and run off together to get married. Between the old folktales of Romeo and Juliet, and the numerous tales of gods and goddesses doing reckless things in the name of love, this was understood to be a normal part of life.

Folklore about Future Spouses

Each Italian girl would have a chosen saint, as well as the Virgin Mary, to whom she would pray. She would often pray to her saint or to Mary for a strong, honorable, industrious man who would care for her and her family for years to come.

The gods and goddesses also had their influence on the Italians. There were many who also prayed to Venus, the Roman goddess of love, to bring them romance and passion. As Venus' symbols were the rose, myrtle, and doves, people would often involve these symbols or items in their lives to encourage love.

The Italians considered turquoise to be a love charm. It is even used in the play The Merchant of Venice by Shakespeare in this manner. If you are trying to catch the attention of someone, try giving them an object with turquoise in it!

One Roman tradition stems from worship of the goddess Pomona, who watched over orchards. A tub of water would be set out, and an apple would be put into it for each potential suitor. The number of bites it took to bring up a given apple would indicate how deeply in love the woman would be with that man. You might recognize this as the current Halloween tradition we have of bobbing for apples!

Another tradition involved walnuts. To the Italians, walnuts were a sign of fertility. Two walnuts would be put into the embers of a fire. If they cracked cleanly into two pieces with a loud noise, this was a sign of a strong, lasting love. If they cracked into tiny pieces or made no noise, this was a sign of a weak love, with disastrous results.

The History of Choosing a Proper Spouse

As far back as the days of the Roman Empire and medieval Italy, a match was about the dispersal of land and the joining of families. While a man and woman without any land to their name might choose who they wished to marry, any situation which involved property and rank became the domain of the fathers. They would want to ensure that their rank was not harmed, and hopefully was improved by the match.

Virginity in a girl was extremely important. For this reason, many families would marry a girl off as young as 12 or 13, as soon as she reached puberty, to ensure that she was safely in the hands of her husband before anything untoward could happen to her. She was also more manageable at this age, and less likely to refuse the match.

The Process of Mate-Choosing

Usually the father of the intended groom would initiate the contact with the father of the bride. If the groom was an older man, he might initiate that contact himself. He would present his case, explaining his own rank and wealth, and express his interest in the bride. The two men would then begin a series of careful negotiations, to determine just how much of a dowry was necessary to seal the transaction, and if the resulting 'merger' of the two families would be to the benefit of both.

Rarely would the woman instigate the match in any way, and often she was not involved until the later stages of the engagement process. However, most caring fathers would take her wishes into account, and look for a husband who would care for her and encourage her interests in life. The girl would pray for such a match, and look forward to doing her duty for her family.

An Italian Proposal

Make haste slowly.

—Italian Proverb

With a culture so steeped in tradition, religion, and marriage, you can imagine that an official proposal is a highly venerated act. It has to be done properly, with all steps done in the correct order, and should be done with great respect, romance, and elegance.

Two peasants who had no land or property might be able to marry without parental involvement at all, beyond the honorary request for the girl's hand. The more property and land that was involved, the more intricate the process became. For pairings involving more wealthy families, where large amounts of land and money were at stake, the engagement process would be split into four distinct parts: the impalmamento, the sponsalia, the matrimonium, and the nozze.

Proposing the Italian Way

Many, many marriages in Italy were arranged. The families would wish to solidify their relationship with each other, or ensure the continued strength of the family. The handshake between the two fathers which sealed this deal was called the "impalmamento". This was the legal agreement between the two families that the marriage would occur.

Often a young girl was promised before she turned 13, and a formal arrangement was made for the pair. The parents would approve the union, and sometimes the two children would even be 'married' legally. They would not be expected to actually live with one another and fulfill the role of man and wife until they were much older.

Even today, some marriages are arranged by a matchmaker, the "sensale", who works to find appropriate brides for the men who employ her. When a match seems suitable, the matchmaker will send a message, or "masciata", to the father of the bride.

In more recent times in Italy, the majority of marriages involve a man who chooses a bride of his own free will. After he has courted the woman in proper fashion for many months, he goes to the home of the woman's family to formally ask her father for her hand in marriage, presenting the diamond ring. The traditional day for engagements is still St. Valentine's Day.

The Families Begin Their Research

However the match was initiated, the parents of the couple would thoroughly investigate each other's families. To the Italians, it was actually the two families that would be joining together, not just the two married people. This process could take several weeks to several months as they found time to get together and debated the merits of the match.

The bride's family was usually expected to pay a handsome dowry to the groom's family, and this would be a key part of the discussions. The bride's family would argue that she was very fertile, would have many children, and would be an excellent housekeeper. The groom's family would argue that she would spend a lot of money, require much clothing, and that they should be paid to take her off of the bride's parents' hands.

Particulars of money and land changing hands would not be discussed yet. The main issue was the 'suitability of the match' – discerning whether the arrangement would benefit both families, either in rank, land, or wealth.

If the families decided that the union was not in their best interest, the marriage would be called off. This could be done up until the final handshake ("impalmamento") with no shame to either side. It was expected that both families would do extremely due diligence before giving their final approval. However, once that handshake had taken place, any deviation from the agreement could lead to a fierce feud, if not an all out familial war.

The Match is Approved

Once the two families approved of the union, the boy and girl could finally meet. Italian women were fiercely protected and were often not allowed out in public. Their world was the inner courtyard and rooms of their home. For the meeting, she would be allowed to lean out of her window (on the second floor) and talk to him. She would sometimes throw a token of her affection down to him, and he would bring gifts with him that he would present to the mother or father.

It was considered good form and their duty for the boy and girl to try to get to know each other and to become friendly. Only if the bride protested fiercely would the father consider calling off the match. As a dutiful daughter, it was her responsibility to do what best suited the family. She would know her place, while still looking forward hopefully to the future.

It was during this stage that the man would formally present his fiancée with her engagement ring.

Italian Engagements

The Rings

Jewelry has always been full of symbolism in Italy. Lovers' rings with inscriptions on the inside have been found dating back to the days of the Romans. Fancy brooches, rings, and necklaces are often found in archaeological digs. The engagement ring—perhaps one of the most important rings in a man or woman's full life, was a vital part of the marriage process.

Gold was always the currency of Rome. Engagement rings were therefore made of gold, to show the great value the groom placed on the upcoming wedding and his bride. The stone itself was less important—diamonds only came into fashion in the last few hundred years. The groom might choose a stone which matched her eyes, or which symbolized the colors of either family. When diamonds became popular, they were said to be the 'flames of love'. Many couples would choose other stones, though, to make their ring a unique symbol for their own special love.

Here are some words and phrases traditionally inscribed on the inner side of a lover's ring or engagement ring:

beautiful: bello
darling: tesoro
dear: caro
loyalty: lealta
love: amore
sweetheart: inamorato
I love you: ti amo

The Financial Arrangements

The second stage of a formal Italian engagement was the "sponsalia". This is when the males in the two families got down to the actual financial discussions. Every detail would be evaluated. The men would evaluate the precise items in the bride's hope chest and the dowry the bride's family would give to the groom. They would evaluate any land and possessions transferred between the two families as part of the arrangement. They would also count any changes in title or rank that the union would cause.

At times there were stipulations that some of the dowry money could be used by the bride for her own clothing, but most of the time it was given to the groom to use at his discretion. The bride was to be taken care of by the groom, and the family wealth was in his hands. This process could take several months to finalize, before both families were satisfied with the results. Once an agreement had been reached, documents would be drawn up describing exactly what money and land was to change hands, on what dates. Signatures would be put down, legally indicating the groom and both fathers promised to hold up their ends of the bargain.

Note that the bride and female relations did not take part in any of this. This was solely an arrangement between the men of the family.

The details of the marriage were now arranged. The next two stages of the marriage, the matrimonium and the nozze, involved the actual signing of the vows and did not take place until the end of the process.

Italian Engagement Traditions

Every Italian girl was brought up to dream of her wedding day. Weddings were family affairs, with everyone getting involved in the planning and preparation. Young girls would help make the wedding foods and sew the dresses,dreaming of the day when it would be their turn.

While to the men, weddings were about land and wealth, women often focused on the religious aspect of the wedding. For both the religious and transactional reasons, weddings were very public and visible. News of the wedding would be announced many times by the church and published in the local newspapers. Both families involved would want to make sure that this merger, and all it meant as far as land, status and reputation went, was well known.

The Hope Chest

Part of an Italian girl's preparation for her wedding was the "hope chest". This wooden trunk, called a "trousseau" from the original French word, was given to a girl when she was very young. The chest would store all of the things she would need as a married woman, from wedding items to household items to clothes for her future husband. It was always assumed that she would, of course, get married as soon as she was of the right age. The girl would receive gifts over the years that were meant to go into this chest.

Note that the bride would be expected to bring these things into her married life along with a substantial dowry from her family. So filling the chest with quality items was a duty for the family, and would reflect as much on them as on the girl when the wedding was planned.

Choosing a Wedding Date

Italians were very religious, but they were also extremely superstitious. They felt strongly that the omens had to be right for a marriage to be successful. Also, they felt that a wedding was an extremely serious step, and should never be rushed. A wedding should be properly planned, announced well in advance, and then accomplished slowly and properly.

An Italian wedding should never be held during Lent, for that would interfere with the enjoyment of the celebration. Weddings were not to be held during Advent because no other thoughts should interfere with the worship of the Advent. They were forbidden during May, because this month was dedicated to the Virgin Mary. They were also avoided during August, because an August wedding was simply bad luck.

Because of their strong religious feelings, Sunday was the perfect day for a wedding—it meant that you could go to church once in the morning, and then go back again later for the ceremony. A marriage on Sunday was supposed to bring great luck to the couple. Note that this is a marked difference from other cultures who feel that Sunday is explicitly a day of rest, and that no celebrations should take place on that day.

Because the morning mass was attended by all, most weddings were held in the late morning or early afternoon on a Sunday.

The Italian Wedding Invitation

Italians were lovers of art and culture and fine writing. The Italian wedding invitation would be hand calligraphed on fine parchment, and decorated with drawn flowers or scrollwork. Roses would be very appropriate.

Emphasizing the family nature of the wedding would be key in an Italian style invitation, with the names of both families and the parents of both individuals listed prominently. The family coat of arms or colors would be incorporated into the invitation design if possible.

If you want to evoke the beauty and honor of an Italian wedding, a beautiful Italian invitation can be hand-written on parchment scrolls, tied with ribbon, and mailed in mailing tubes to the welcome guests.

Italian Wedding Blessings and Sayings

With the importance placed on religion in Italy, and the sacredness of the wedding vows, blessings would be very appropriate as part of an invitation set, and would have an important role in any Italian wedding ceremony.

Heavenly Father,

we praise you for your wisdom

in arranging that man should not be alone but should unite himself to another

to form a living cell or unit,

bringing forth new members for your kingdom.

And he answered and said unto them, Have ye not read, that he which made them at the beginning made

them male and female,

And said, For this cause shall a man leave father and mother, and shall cleave to his wife: and they

twain shall be one flesh?

Wherefore they are no more twain, but one flesh. What therefore God hath joined together, let not

man put asunder.

This is probably the most famous blessing of them all, used at many Italian weddings, from 1 Corinthians 13:

If I speak in the tongues of men and of angels, but have not love, I am only a resounding gong or a clanging cymbal.

If I have the gift of prophecy and can fathom all mysteries and all knowledge, and if I have a faith that can move mountains, but have not love, I am nothing.

If I give all I possess to the poor and surrender my body to the flames, but have not love, I gain nothing.

Love is patient, love is kind. It does not envy, it does not boast, it is not proud.

It is not rude, it is not self-seeking, it is not easily angered, it keeps no record of wrongs.

Love does not delight in evil but rejoices with the truth.

It always protects, always trusts, always hopes, always perseveres.

Love never fails. But where there are prophecies, they will cease; where there are tongues, they will be stilled; where there is knowledge, it will pass away.

For we know in part and we prophesy in part, but when perfection comes, the imperfect disappears.

When I was a child, I talked like a child, I thought like a child, I reasoned like a child. When I became a man, I put childish ways behind me.

Now we see but a poor reflection as in a mirror; then we shall see face to face. Now I know in part; then I shall know fully, even as I am fully known.

And now these three remain: faith, hope and love. But the greatest of these is love.

A pair of blessings that might be used at the wedding feast:

Signore del mondo,

il pane della terra ci sostiene,

il vino rallegra il nostro cuore e l'olio illumina il nostro volto.

Sii benedetto per queste creature, doni preziosi che vengono da te per la consolazione di noi uomini.

Translation:

Lord of the World,

bread from the earth sustains us wine gladdens our heart

and oil makes our faces shine.

May you be blessed for these creatures precious gifts that come from you

for the comfort of us human beings

✝ ✝ ✝

O Dio,

che ci concedi ogni giorno il pane, il vino, e l'olio

saziandoci nella tua benevolenza. benedici questo nostro stare a mensa e donaci la gratitudine verso di te e verso tutta la creazione Translation:

O God,

every day you give us bread, wine, and oil

satisfying us with your generosity. Bless our being together at this table and give us gratitude toward you and toward all of creation.

Note that if your wedding is a Roman Catholic one, you can get an official blessing from the Pope, to frame and hang on your wall. You'll need to speak with the Chancellor or Chancery office of your Diocese to get the appropriate forms, and it can take up to six months to process. Well worth the wait, this can be a truly special way to celebrate your special day for the rest of your lives.

Italian Sayings

Italians have many folk sayings about weddings and marriage. As marriage is a much celebrated part of life, most speak of the importance of that bond and its power.

Dating:

Il primo amore non si scorda mai.

You never forget your first love.

Bacco, tabacco e Venere riducono l'uomo in cenere

Wine, women, and tobacco can ruin a man.

In amore è in guerra tutto è lecito

All's fair in love and war.

Wedding:

Sposa bagnata, sposa fortunata

Rain on a bride's wedding day is good luck.

Dio li fa e poi li accoppia.

God makes them, and then joins them.

Matrimoni e viscuvati, di lu celu su mannati.

Weddings and spiritual matters are heaven sent.

Moglie e buoi dei paesi tuoi.

Marry a woman from your own neighborhood.

Marriage:

La buona moglie fa il buon marito

A good wife makes a good husband.

La moglie è la chiave di casa.

A good wife is the key to a good home.

Tra moglie e marito ... non mettere il dito.

Don't put a finger between wife and husband.

Casa senza fimmina 'mpuvirisci

A house without a woman is poor.

Lo specchio migliore è il viso dell'amico

The best mirror is the face of a friend.

Amor nuovo va e viene, amore vecchio si mantiene

New love goes and comes, old love is maintained.

La tavola e il letto mantien l'affetto.

The table and the bed maintain the affection.

A ogni uccello il suo nido è bello.

To every bird, his own nest is beautiful.

Meglio il marito senz'amore, che con gelosia.

Better to have a husband without love than one who is jealous.

Ne di Venere ne di Marte non si sposa ne si parte!

Neither marriage nor war will go away once begun.

The Matrimonium

About a week before the wedding came the third stage in the official Italian engagement process. This was when all final arrangements were complete as far as the agreements regarding land and wealth go. Both families would meet at the bride's home in front of a town clerk. He would first verify that both the bride and groom were old enough to marry, that the families were in full consent, and that there was no legal impediment to the union. Next, proof would be offered that all financial and land-related tasks had been completed to everyone's satisfaction.

The couple would then agree to marry. The two would don their best clothes, but again this was a legal ceremony so there was not a lot of extra decoration or dress-up involved. The bride would leave her hair down as she was not yet becoming a church-blessed wife. The groom would vow to care for his wife. The bride would vow to obey and serve her new husband. They would exchange rings, and they would now be legally married. They could not yet live together or consummate the marriage however—this would have to wait for the full church wedding.

This is similar to the 'civil wedding' required in most locations today, to make a wedding legal and to consummate the financial transactions between the families.

Often, the bride and groom would give each other small presents on this day as well. One tradition was for the bride to be given a "bridal belt". These belts were long, made of sumptuous fabrics and often contained intricate embroidery or metalwork. This custom traces back to the god Vulcan giving such a belt to his love, Venus. Note that Venus' day was February 14th! The worship of Venus was very strong, and it is said that even Julius Caesar had a battle-cry of 'Venus among us!'

The Night Before the Wedding

The night before the wedding was the last evening before a serious commitment, and both the bride and groom took this step with a great deal of thought. There were no wild parties, no drunken acts. Both the bride and groom had a great deal of respect for each other and would want this final night to show their best form, truly deserving of one another.

The bride would wear green on this last evening, to bring her luck and fertility. She would take a long bath to wash away her worries, often scented with rose petals.

The evening would feature prayers for the success of the marriage, a final large meal with their families, and much talking into the evening. It would end with a good night's sleep so that they could be fresh and ready for the long day ahead.

An Italian Wedding

Matrimoni e vescovati sono dal cielo destinati.

Marriages are made in heaven.

—Italian proverb

A wedding in Italy is perhaps the most important event that happens in a community. It is the continuation of that community, a bond that is expected to lead to children and to new generations to share in the

community's traditions. It doesn't just involve the two people being married, but their entire families as well.

In a formal Italian wedding, this stage was the "Nozze". This was where the bride officially went to live with the groom and the marriage could be consummated. Sometimes over a year would pass between the legal signing of the marriage documents and the actual wedding. If the couple was young, several years might pass.

If you are looking for a good portrayal in the movies of what an Italian wedding would be like, rent the movie "The Godfather". While other scenes may be a bit violent, watch for the wedding scene set in Italy. This is well done, and was portrayed in the true authentic Sicilian style.

Heading to the Church

Most families in Italy were not very wealthy, and it was expected that the families would walk to church. To show his respect, the groom would first walk to the bride's house and greet the family. He would then formally escort his bride and her family to the church.

The village would get involved in this procession, and attempt to challenge the new bride. They might put a crying child in her path, to test her role as a mother. They might leave items out in the path, like a forgotten rake or hoe. The bride would be expected to pick these up and move them out of the way of the procession, to show her skill as a housekeeper. All eyes were on the bride as she proved herself, in these final minutes, as a worthy and well-raised woman.

How she acted reflected not only on her, but on her parents and how they had brought her up.

Some villages became more extreme in their pre-ceremony tests. A few would set up a large log with a double-handed saw. The couple would stand on either side of the log and saw it in half together, showing that they were able to work together and were fit to be proper husband and wife.

The bride would stand at the back of the church as the groom went forward to wait by the altar. Everyone else would be seated before the bride made her formal entrance, with her father. Her father would then walk her down the aisle, often embrace her, then gently place her hand on the groom's, giving him her "hand" in marriage.

Groom Wear

The Italian man would wear his very best outfit, as befitting this important day. Only the most wealthy men would pay for a special outfit for this event. Most men would do the best they could with their finest jacket and pants.

Ever fearful of bad omens, the man would be sure to carry iron (tocca ferro) to ward off the evil eye (mal'occhio). He would wear a boutonniere of the same color and type of flower as carried by his bride in her bouquet. This traces back to the days of knights and chivalry, when a knight would carry a token from his love to show his loyalty to her.

Note that in some villages, the groom's tie would be cut up into pieces, and the pieces sold off as mementos to the guests to help pay for the musicians.

Bridal Wear

As in most cultures, the Italian bride would always wear a veil over her face. This was to show that she was 'unknown to man' (pure) and also to protect her from the evil eye. In addition, because most marriages were arranged, it would help ensure the groom went through with the ceremony regardless of what she looked like. To tear the veil was a sign of good luck.

An Italian bride would often wear a sash around her waist, with knots in it, to keep away the evil spirits. The knots symbolized the commitment of the couple to bind together, that no spirits can pull asunder.

For the Italians, blue was the color of purity and fidelity. That is why you will often see statues of the Virgin Mary in blue, showing that she is ever chaste. White was in fact often a color of death, used at funerals. White only became popular as a sign of virginity with Anne of Brittany in 1499, in France. If the bride did not have a blue dress, she would wear her best dress, whatever color it was.

On this, the most important day in her life, the bride wore no gold until the wedding ring was placed on her finger. The ring therefore took on special significance as the most valuable thing she had. According to Roman tradition, the ring was put on the 3rd finger, because this was the finger most closely connected with the heart.

Herbs were very important to the Italians, far more so than flowers. A bride would typically carry a cloth pouch containing herbs to bring her good fortune. These would include oregano for joy, dill for fertility, and garlic as a protection from evil spirits.

Bridesmaids and Groomsmen

When you look at wedding portraits, you often see that the men all dress very similarly to one another, as do the women. This comes from an ancient Roman tradition. Evil spirits were thought to be jealous of the love of the bride and groom, and would wish to cause trouble for them. The bridesmaids and groomsmen would dress similarly to confuse these spirits, and foil their attempts.

Church Decorations

One of the most visible decorations that signified a wedding in Italy was a large fabric bow across the church door. This was a clear sign to all around that a wedding was taking place inside, that a couple was 'tying the knot'.

The inside of the church was not usually decorated, for this was a solemn religious ceremony. If any flowers were used, often it would be the rose, the traditional Italian flower of love. If the ceremony was held on Palm Sunday, often there would be palm fronds decorating the sanctuary.

The Italian Ceremony

An Italian wedding ceremony would typically be the second religious ceremony of the day. The couple would have already gone to a morning mass, and would now be returning for the late- morning or early afternoon wedding ceremony.

The strong religious fervor of the Italians meant that the wedding ceremony would be very solemn and formal. The priest would remind the couple of the serious oath they were making to each other and to God. God was to be an important part of the marriage. Often the priest would include religious direction to the couple, to educate and encourage them. Wedding ceremonies in Italy were often quite long, sometimes lasting for hours.

The End of the Ceremony

As with most wedding ceremonies, the bride and groom kissed to seal their intentions to each other. In some families, it was the tradition to shatter a glass, to show that their lives before were now over and that they had a new life together. Tradition had it that the number of pieces of glass might represent the number of years they would be happy together.

Other families would release doves to show that a new love was now in the world.

Leaving the Church

These were the first steps that the new couple took as man and wife, and the entire congregation wanted these to be full of love and celebration. Typically, the church would be on one side of the main square in the center of the village. As the couple came down the front steps into the cobblestone square, they would be showered with rice and confetti (small candy-coated almonds). Both were symbols of the new couple's wealth and fertility. Note that while it was rumored that birds would eat rice and their stomachs would explode, this has been found not to be true. So if you wish to enjoy the tradition of rice, go ahead and do so!

In older farming villages, the fertility presents were even more basic. The new couple would be showered with wheat to give them female children, and barley for male children. Walnuts were another sign of fertility, although these would be tossed more gently!

The new couple would stroll out of the church under this shower, and parade around the town square to the applause and cheers of all. They would stop and talk to their neighbors and friends before walking together to where the reception was being held. Often the reception was at the bride's or groom's family's home.

If the family was wealthy, the bride would be lifted onto a white horse. She would then be led in a torch-lit procession to the reception location.

An Italian Reception

A tavola non s'invecchia.

One never gets old at a table.

—Italian proverb

The reception for an Italian wedding would be a huge affair lasting all day and involving most of the local village. It was a chance for the two families to show off their wealth and to celebrate the happiness of the young couple. There would be generous amounts of food available, lots of singing and music, lots of wine and Italian liquor.

Debts would be forgiven, favors would be asked, lavish gifts would be given to the bride and groom. It was not just a celebration for these two individuals, it would be a celebration of life in general, that the cycle of life was continuing.

Traditions for a Happy Marriage

Many wedding traditions in the Italian culture have to do with bringing fertility to the new couple. This was one of the most important things that could be wished for the marriage.

The Italians were full of hope, and many sayings helped encourage the bride even if things seemed unfortunate. For example, if it rained on the couple during their wedding day, this was considered to be a very lucky omen.

A traditional clothing item for a bride was "La Borsa". This was a satin bag that often had a loop on it for her to carry on her wrist. This is how the bride would collect all of the wedding money she was offered throughout the evening. This would represent the couple's ability to gather wealth throughout their life together. This tradition of the bride gathering money is called "buste".

Note that if the groom expects the bride to do this, he should talk with her about it beforehand! To a non-Italian woman, the thought of going around begging for cash at her own wedding may be quite upsetting, and I've heard of this causing serious unhappiness at a wedding when it was a surprise to the bride.

Decorations and Flowers

As mentioned before, flowers were not of great importance to the Italians. They loved fountains and greenery, but would rather have herbs than overflowing bouquets. Roses, however, were the exception, and were often used for these times of love and romance.

For decoration, consider the use of the millefiore—'thousand flowers'—glass style from murano. This famous style is often associated with love.

The Italians were very fond of poetry and song. A common favor at an Italian wedding would be parchment scrolls, with a favorite poem on each, tied with ribbons. You could have the bride and groom sign the bottom of each parchment as a token of their love for their guests.

While the Italians were very formal about the ceremony, the reception was definitely somewhere to enjoy, for the family and friends to get to know one another, in an atmosphere of joy and delight.

For a more intriguing Italian reception, try a masked party! You can see examples of these from Romeo and Juliet, Much Ado about Nothing, and the Taming of the Shrew. All three take place in Italy and show how much the masked party was enjoyed. You could invite guests to bring their own masks, or leave a wide selection of them at the entrance to the reception area.

Italian Music and Dance

The keys to any Italian celebration are song and dance. This is
especially true at a wedding celebration. One of the most famous
Italian dances is "La Tarantella". The name means "Tarantula", like
the spider, and the dance does end up looking like a giant spider's
web.

In essence the dancers form a long single chain, each putting his
hands on the shoulders of the person in front of him. They begin to
dance around in a circle clockwise, as if they were a long snake.
When the music changes, the 'head' of the snake switches directions,
and now starts to dance counter-clockwise. Everyone behind has to
follow along. The music gets faster and faster, and the dance becomes
a giant weaving with people trying to keep up with the various turns.
It is great fun, and tends to bring all celebrants into the dance as it
progresses.

The Italian Wedding Feast

Food is an extremely important part of an Italian wedding. There should be copious amounts of food, of all flavors, shapes, and textures. Nobody should go home even remotely hungry, and many people bring doggie bags home with them. Buffet style is usually best because of the volume of dishes and selections available, so that each person can choose what they want and go back repeatedly to try out other options. There can be upwards of 10 or more courses served, each more lavish than the last.

The Italians love wine, and a good selection of wine would be offered, from the fruity red chiantis to the crisp pinot grigios and sweet proseccos. Whether the guest was currently enjoying a fresh goat cheese, a spicy meatball or a delicate pastry, there would be a wine nearby to help complement that dish.

One of the traditions with serving food at an Italian wedding feast is to serve everything in odd numbers. If there are small bags of candy, they should contain odd numbers of candies. The idea is that nothing is 'evenly divisible' now—everything must be shared between the group.

Meat was the traditional centerpiece of any Italian feast, and the three popular types were roast sheep, sausage, and pig. Some areas had more of a delicacy meat—the roasted baby lamb (bacchio) or roasted baby pig (porchetta). You may want to look into doing a roast of one of these if you have an outdoor wedding in the summer, or you can seek a version which suits your own needs.

Common appetizers would include olives, calamari, stuffed mushrooms, salami and sausage, cheeses of all varieties, and garlic bread.

Stuffed Mushrooms

This is a delicous appetizer for any sort of gathering, and is a favorite at Italian weddings.

1 lb hot Italian sausage
1 onion, finely chopped
1/2 green pepper, finely diced
1/4 tsp garlic powder
1/4 cup dry bread crumbs
1/4 tsp salt
dash of pepper
1 1/4 cups spaghetti sauce
40 large mushroom caps
5 Tbsp olive oil
1 cup mozzarella cheese, shredded

Mix together the sausage, onion, green pepper, and garlic powder. Sauté in a skillet, then drain off the fat. Add in the bread crumbs, salt, pepper, and spaghetti sauce.

Next, coat the mushroom caps with olive oil with a sprayer. Fill the mushroom caps with the meat mixture. Place the caps with their cups facing up onto a cookie sheet, cover with foil, and bake at 350□F for 20 minutes.

Sprinkle the caps with mozzarella cheese, then broil until cheese is melted and mushrooms are tender.

A soave would go well with this dish.

Fried Calamari

Calamari, or squid, is a traditional Italian dish. Don't be shy about trying this dish – it's really quite tasty!

12 ounces fresh calamari
3/4 cup olive oil
2 Tbsp parsley
clove garlic
tsp marjoram
salt and pepper
rice
flour
oil for frying

First, you need to prepare the calamari. Note that if you do not wish to prepare it yourself, you can purchase it already prepared at many stores. First remove the innards, then remove the quill and peel away the skin. Now cut the head off and remove the mouth. Wash the tentacles and body. Cut the body into ring shapes, about 1/4" wide. The tentacles are fine as they are.

For the marinade, add in the olive oil, parsley, garlic, marjoram, salt and pepper. Mix, then add in the calamari. Let it soak for an hour in the fridge.

Pour frying oil into a deep pan until the oil is 2" deep. Now heat the oil until dropping in a drop of water causes it to bubble. Shake off the marinade and roll the rings in the flour until coated. Now cook the rings until they turn golden brown. Remove the rings with a slotted spoon, and then lay on paper towels.

Pinot Grigio goes nicely with calamari.

Tomato-Cheese Torte

Tortes are always very popular at Italian weddings. This one is simple to make and highlights some of the traditional ingredients used in Italian cooking.

16 oz cream cheese
2 cloves garlic, minced
3 oz sun dried tomatoes
8 oz pesto
10 slices provolone cheese

Mix together garlic and cream cheese. Boil 2 cups of water, then reduce to a simmer. Add in tomatoes and cook for 5 minutes. Chop the tomatoes into small cubes.

To begin the torte assembly, line a bowl with a cheese cloth. First add in a layer of the provolone cheese. Put in half of the pesto. Next add in half of the garlic blend. Add in half of the tomatoes.

Next, another layer of provolone, then another layer of pesto, more garlic blend, and more tomatoes. Top it with the final layer of provolone cheese. Wrap the cheesecloth across the top to cover it.

Refrigerate for 4 hours, then invert onto a plate to serve. Serve with a fruity chianti.

Italian Wedding Soup

Wedding soup can be found at just about any traditional Italian wedding. It is made fresh, so bowls of the soup can be laid out on a table for guests to come and retrieve as it's ready. In keeping with the Italian traditions of indivisibility, each bowl should have an odd number of meatballs in it.

8 cups chicken broth
3/4 pound ground pork
3/4 pound ground beef
1 cup dry bread crumbs
3 eggs
2 teaspoons dried basil
1 teaspoon dried parsley
1/2 cup grated Parmesan
2 medium heads escarole

Topping: 5 eggs
1 cup grated Parmesan

Boil the broth. While it is coming to a boil, mix together the pork, beef, bread crumbs, eggs, basil, parsley, and parmesan cheese. Form the mixture into small meatballs about ½" across. Add them into the boiling broth.

Now clean and chop the escarole, and add it in. Cook for 7 minutes.

For the topping, blend together the 5 eggs with the cup of grated cheese. When the main soup is done, slowly stir the topping in for about a minute. Serve promptly.

Wedding soup can be enjoyed with a crisp pinot grigio.

An Italian Wedding Cake

Italy is a culture with a long tradition of beauty and sculpture. The Italian fascination with beauty values it so strongly, it is well worth any wait. The wedding cake is no exception.

The tradition of the wedding cake originated in ancient Rome. Bread has always been seen as a symbol of fertility, and after the wedding the bride would have a thin cake broken on her head to bring her fertility. The guests would then gather up the crumbs to share in her good fortune. As the years passed, the cake became a cake for eating, and the guests would partake along with the couple. The brilliant chefs of Italy worked to make the wedding cake a crowning triumph of the wedding feast.

The cake should be elegant and rich, beautifully decorated and full of interesting ingredients. The classic white cake would often have unexpected items like nuts and pineapple in it. These ingredients would both pique the interest of the guests and show the wealth and good taste of the bride and groom.

Italian Wedding Cake Recipe

For the Italians, a wedding cake should both look beautiful and taste delicious. If the bride does not enjoy some of these ingredients, substitute in ones she does enjoy. For the decorations, incorporate roses, doves, and other symbols of love.

Cake:
1/2 cup buttermilk
1 tsp salt
1 tsp baking soda
2 cups white sugar
1/2 cup butter
1/2 cup shortening
 5 egg yolks
tsp vanilla extract
1/4 tsp almond extract
cups all-purpose flour
5 egg whites
1 cup chopped pecans
1/2 cup flaked coconut
1/2 cup drained crushed pineapple

Frosting:
4 cups confectioners' sugar
1 cup chopped pecans
3/4 cup butter, softened
8 oz package cream cheese, softened
2 tsp vanilla extract

Blend together the buttermilk, salt, and baking soda.

Separately, blend the sugar, butter, and shortening. Add in the yolks slowly to the sugar mixture, then the vanilla and almond. Next add in the buttermilk mixture, then the flour.

In a new bowl, beat the egg whites until it forms peaks. Fold the eggs into the batter, and gently add in the pecans, coconut and pineapple.

Grease and flour three 8" cake pans, and split the batter evenly between these three. Bake the cake at 350°F for 30 minutes. Test the cake with a toothpick before removing it. The cake is done when a toothpick inserted in the center comes out clean. Cool completely before frosting.

For the frosting, blend together all ingredients listed until smooth. Frost and then decorate extravagantly, using traditional symbols such as doves and roses.

Coffee in Italy

No Italian festivities would be complete without an ending of rich coffee and pastries. Coffee is a long-standing Italian tradition. It was first enjoyed in the late 1500s, and by the early 1600s advisors tried to convince Pope Clement VIII to ban coffee because it came from the Ottoman Empire. However, the Pope could not stand to part with his favorite drink, and he instead approved it, so that Christians could now enjoy it without its heathen connotations.

By 1645, coffeehouses were opening all over Italy, and the morning cup of coffee became part of the culture.

In addition to regular coffee, Italy is also known for two special styles of coffee—espresso and cappuccino.

Espresso

Espresso is a distinctly Italian form of coffee. The name is a short form of "espressamente per lei", meaning "expressly for you". Where coffee was usually brewed in quantity, espresso was hand made for each customer.

The Espresso machine was designed and patented in the early 1900s. Luigi Bezzera ran a factory, and coffee breaks were hurting his productivity. He had an inventive mind, and began working on how to get coffee brewed more quickly, so that he could get his employees to work more. He pressurized the brewing process to speed it up, and found that the quality of the flavor also improved. While his new espresso was a hit, he wasn't very good at marketing and, sadly, died a pauper.

Achilles Gaggie's updated version of the machine came out in the 1940's, and quickly became very popular. The drink is now known world wide, and appreciated for its delicious aroma and flavor.

Cappuccino

Cappuccino gets its name from its color—it is the same shade as robes worn by the Capuchin order of monks. It begins with a base of espresso. The correct proportions for true cappuccino are:

One third espresso

One third steamed milk

One third milk foam

The drink is then sprinkled with cocoa powder for a hint of chocolate.

If you are a devoted fan of chocolate, try a "mochaccino". That's a cappuccino with chocolate flavoring added.

Italian Wedding Pastries

meglio un giorno da leoni che cento anni da pecora.

Better to live a day like a lion than a century like a sheep.

—Italian proverb

Pastries are the highlight of any Italian wedding feast, and go perfectly with all of the coffees that Italians love so much. Even young Italian women who were obsessed with their shapely figure would enjoy all delicacies on this celebratory day, to share in the joy of the new couple.

Often there is a special table set aside for all of these pastries and cookies, conveniently located near the coffee station. Some weddings even feature a 'pastry dance' where the new couple starts a tarantella, and dances past the pastry table. Each guest picks up a treat as they go.

Bomboniera

These items are now popular at any type of wedding, but the origin is Italian. Bomboniera are colored sugar-coated almonds distributed in small bags of tulle fabric. The bags-with-almond packages are called 'bomboniera', while the individual almonds within are called "confetti". The almonds should be bagged in odd numbers for good luck, so that they cannot be easily divided. The almonds are thought to bring fertility to the couple, and their sweet outside and bitter inside shows that every relationship survives with some good and some bad.

Depending on the wedding, these bags can be provided for each guest at their plate, or sometimes the bride distributes them by hand, to share her sweet new life with each guest.

Biscotti

One of Italy's favorite treats is biscotti, which is a hard cookie perfect for dunking in coffee.

3 cups flour
1 cup sugar
4 eggs
1/4 cup olive oil
1/4 cup sliced almonds
2 tsp vanilla
2 tsp almond extract
2 tsp baking powder

Sift the flour, then blend in the rest of the ingredients until it reaches a doughy consistency. Knead the dough until it is smooth, adding more flour if necessary.

Split the dough into two pieces, and roll each piece out to about 12" by 4". Put each rectangle onto a greased cookie sheet. Bake at 350°F for 20 minutes. Cut into pieces about 4" by 1/2" and then flip them over. Cook them for another 3 minutes at 425°F for the final toasting. Serve cool.

Wanda

These bowtie shaped pastry are a classic at any Italian wedding. They are thought to bring good luck and fertility to the new couple.

6 large eggs
1/3 cup sugar
1/3 cup butter
1 tsp vanilla
4 to 6 cups flour
tsp baking powder
1/2 tsp salt
quarts cooking oil

Icing
1/2 lb powdered sugar
1/2 tsp vanilla
2 Tbsp melted butter
1 Tbsp milk

Mix together the eggs, sugar, butter, and vanilla until smooth.

In a separate bowl, mix together the flour, baking powder, and salt. Combine the two together and mix until it forms a dough.

Knead the dough until it forms a smooth ball, adding in additional flour if necessary to get a smooth texture. Put the dough into a greased bowl and cover it with a towel for 15 minutes at room temperature

Split the dough into 10 balls. As you work on each ball, keep the rest covered. Knead each ball for 5 minutes.

Split the ball into thirds. Roll each piece into thin strips with a rolling pin. With a fluted cutter, trim the dough into strips of 9" long by 3/4" wide. Twist them into bowtie shapes.

Repeat until all dough balls have been made into bowties.

Heat the oil in a deep pan. It should be about 2" deep. Drop in a bit of flour to test the heat of the oil. If it bubbles, you can begin.

Add several bowties and cook for about 30 seconds on the first side, then flip for another 15 seconds.

Remove with a slotted spoon and drain on a paper towel. Allow to cool thoroughly. Proceed with cooking all of the wanda in small batches.

Mix together all ingredients of the icing until smooth. Use a fork to drizzle the frosting over the top of the cooled pastries, and allow to harden. Store in waxed paper.

Italian Filled Wedding Cookies

These cookies require effort, but they are a delicious complement to any wedding's dessert tray.

5 large eggs
1 1/4 cups sugar
1/2 cup vegetable oil
1 tsp salt
1 tsp vanilla
1 oz light rum
6 cups flour
4 tsp baking powder

8 oz pineapple preserves
1/4 cup coconut flakes

Blend together the eggs and sugar. Now mix in the oil, salt, and vanilla. Mix in the flour and baking powder. Knead the mixture until it forms a dough.

Press the dough into the shape of small pastry cups. Blend together the pineapple preserves and coconut, and put some into each cup. Cook at 375°F for 15 minutes, until lightly browned.

Italian Toasts and Drinks

Champagne and Asti Spumanti

Bubbly is always expected during a celebration. You can go with the Italian bubbly—Asti Spumanti—which is foamy and sweet. You can also go with French Champange, which has been used in celebrations since the 1800's.

Here is a step-by-step guide on how to properly open a bottle of Champagne. Remember, your primary goal in opening a bottle of Champagne is to control the cork and, of course, not to let much of the drink spill.

Every bottle of Champagne or sparkling wine (with a few low-end exceptions) has foil wrapped around the outside of the cork. In the old days, some foil was lead-lined to keep mice from eating into the cork, but this is no longer the case.

From this point onward, keep the cork pointed in a safe direction, and keep one thumb on it, just in case. Corks can loosen over time, so even if you think you're not ready to pop the cork yet, the bottle may have a different idea.

Untwist and remove the wire cage. This cage ensures that the cork does not pop out of the bottle until you are ready to have it do so. Loosen it gently, being sure to keep a thumb on the cork to prevent it from flying out prematurely.

Most people put a towel over the cork at this point, to help control the cork's exit from the bottle.

Hold the cork in one hand (under a towel), and the base of the bottle in the other. Turn the bottle, not the cork, slowly and gently. You want the cork to ease off with a soft "whoof", not a loud pop.

By gently removing the cork, you have saved the bubbles and air from being immediately lost (never mind the Champagne!). Still, with the pressure removed, you should now quickly pour it out for consumption. Slide the towel around to the neck of the bottle for pouring.

You will find that a quick turn of the bottle when you're done pouring each glass will catch the drops on the edge of the lip. Pour the Champagne down the sides of the glasses to minimize foam and therefore bubble waste.

The glasses are poured! Raise them, and give a toast to celebrate!

Never use a corkscrew on a bottle of Champagne! The bottle is under strong pressure and could explode.

Toasts

The traditional toast at a wedding reception is: evviva gli sposi

This means "hurray for the newlyweds!" The guests should cheer wildly when this toast is made.

Another more general toast is: Cent Anni

This toast means "100 years of happiness". There is of course the traditional "kiss the bride!" call, where the guests demand a bit of affection between the pair, either with words, or by clinking their cutlery gently on their glasses.

The Clinking of Glasses during a Toast

As with many food traditions, the clinking of glasses traces its root to the health and safety of the drinker. In this case, it goes back to the tendency of nobles to kill each other by poisoning their food!

Wine was very commonly drunk during medieval days because it was one of the only safe liquids available. Water was often polluted, and milk was both useful for other things and thought to be for children only. As the wine was often full of sediment, a poison was easily introduced into it.

To prove that his wine was safe, the host would pour a bit of his guest's wine into his own glass and drink it first, to prove it was safe. If the guest trusted his host, however, he would merely clink his flagon against that of his host's when his host offered his cup for the sample. The 'clink' (or perhaps 'clunk' back then, since wood or metal was more common for drinking vessels) was a sign of trust and honesty.

Later, as metal and glass became more common, the chiming noise also brought a festive feel to events, and brought to mind the 'safe' feeling of church bells.

Italian Wedding Reception Traditions

Note that although modern Italian couples toast with Champagne, or sometimes Asti Spumanti, in the past the toast was done with a liqueur. As the festivities were getting started, the best man would circulate, offering the guests various liqueurs. Women would be offered sweet liqueurs, while men would be offered the stronger varieties. These would then be used for any toasts.

Here are some traditional liqueurs to try during your Italian celebrations.

Anisette

Anisette is a clear liqueur that is made from anise seeds. It has a licorice flavor. It is a sweeter form of the liqueur "Anis", which is less well known. A common way for the coffee-loving Italians to enjoy Anisette is in a cup of coffee.

Anisette Coffee

½ oz. gin

¾ oz anisette

5 oz. hot coffee

Add all ingredients to a heated mug. Garnish with a lemon twist and add cream or sugar if desired.

Amaretto

Amaretto is made from apricot pits. It is a dark brown color and has a nutty flavor. The most common Amaretto brand is Amaretto di Saronno Originale, with its distinctive square top bottle. Amaretto Sour is one of the most common ways to serve amaretto.

Amaretto Sour

1 1/2 oz. Amaretto

3/4 oz Lemon Juice

2 tsp. Sugar

Mix all ingredients, shake well with cracked ice. Strain into a sour glass. Garnish with a slice of orange.

Grappa

Grappa is a traditional Italian brandy, made from the leftover skins and seeds of the grapes used for wine. The resourceful Italians let nothing go to waste! It was first created in Venice and Tuscany, both large wine producing areas, in the 1400's.

The unused parts of the grape, left behind during winemaking, are called the "Pomacy" or "Pomace". The Pomace is fermented and distilled in its natural state. The resulting liquid is around 90 proof (45% alcohol) and clear in color.

Grappa is also known by other names. It is called Marc in France, Aguardiente in Spain and Portugal, and in Germany it's known as Tresterschnapps.

The grappa is a dry liqueur and high in alcohol content, with flavors ranging from floral to earthy. The taste can have highlights of oak or juniper berries as well. Grappa is typically enjoyed after dinner. You should avoid the giant brandy-snifter glasses that were popular in olden days. Current research shows that brandies, including grappa, are best enjoyed in small glasses.

Sambuca

Sambuca is another licorice flavored liqueur, with a clear color and sweet flavor. This drink is made from witch elder bush and licorice. The flavor tends to be less sweet than anisette and have a higher alcohol level. Sambuca is often served chilled, and can even be enjoyed straight out of the freezer.

Flaming Sambuca

Be sure someone sober is doing the pouring for this! Pour a double shot of sambuca, then add in 5 drops of blue curacao. Put a coaster over the top of the glass so the fumes collect over the liqueur. Lift the coaster, light the alcohol fumes, then drink! Prepare and consume at your own risk.

Almond Delight

Mix 1 shot sambuca with 2 shots of amaretto. Serve with ice.

Aᖴᴛᴇʀ ᴛʜᴇ Rᴇᴄᴇᴘᴛɪᴏɴ

The Italian reception would usually last until the wee hours of the morning if not into the next day. The event was seen as a village party, and little thought was given to the couple's wanting to be alone. They would have enough time to be alone together for the rest of their lives!

When the party finally wound down, the new couple would usually walk to their new home. If the couple drove home, the front of their car would be decorated with flowers, to pave their way with good luck and happiness.

It was bad luck for the bride to trip over the threshold, and this was also where evil spirits would linger, so the groom would carry his new bride into the home. She would often rub wool and oil along the door frame, to show that she was now the woman of the home.

Now that the reception was complete, and the guests were sure to have enjoyed a great deal of liquor, wine, and asti spumanti. This is when the hijinks would begin. The family and friends would often have surprises waiting for the new couple—anything from boarding up the door to the house, to putting candies or herbs in the bed, to making loud noise or serenading the couple from outside their windows. This good-natured ribbing was expected!

The next day, the women in the groom's family would come by to visit the bride and welcome her into their family. They would bring her rings that they themselves had been given when they were new brides. She would now be expected to keep these and pass them along to the brides of her own sons, and to the brides of any nephews in the family. Often the bride's family would also stop by, and give presents to the groom, including items with both families' coats of arms on them.

One Italian custom is that the new husband and wife do not open their own gifts. The pile of presents is left behind while the two go off on their honeymoon. When they return, they'll find the presents laid out by their friends and family, and a list of the presents and their givers.

That makes it easy for the new couple to begin enjoying their presents immediately, and to easily write out thank you cards.

An Italian Honeymoon

Italians loved to travel, and a honeymoon was a well-enjoyed part of many wedding plans. A poor couple might just travel along the local winery trail, tasting as they went, and enjoying the fresh food and wine. A couple with more money might sign on for a month long cruise, visiting the ports of the Mediterranean and enjoying their time together.

Add some Italian touches to your honeymoon! If there are wineries in the area you will visit, stop in to do some tasting. Be sure to check even if it seems unlikely – wineries can now be found in all 50 US states, and in practically every country on earth.

If you have a bit more money, take a cruise trip, enjoying Italian meals when you can. The Italians love the water and any boat- related activity will bring that to mind.

If you can afford it, why not honeymoon in Italy? This is the classic honeymoon destination, from the canals of Venice to the wineries of Tuscany.

Living and Loving the Italian Way

It is easy to bring Italian style into your life! There are so many beautiful posters and prints to hang on your walls, sculptures to decorate your shelves, and pottery and glassware for your kitchen. Most homes probably have an Italian touch or two in them already! Here are some suggestions to bring part of the

Italian culture to your corner of the world.

Italian Touches for your Life

Probably the single most important influence on Italian life is religion. Most Italian homes have a photo or statue of the Virgin Mary, as well as other saints that are important to their life.

Artwork by the Italian masters—Leonardo daVinci and Michelangelo come to mind—would also bring an artistic flair to your world.

Italy was very much about family. Fill your home with family photos, including any old photos you have of your grandparents or great-grandparents. Research your family coat of arms and display it proudly. You can even chart your family tree!

Italian Hobbies to Enjoy

Italians are, by nature, hard working, but they also enjoy their time off. Try these Italian hobbies and see if they suit you as well!

Cooking

Food is integral to the Italian culture. Learn new Italian recipes, and take a course at a local community college to learn new techniques. Not only will you be connecting with an important aspect of Italian life, but your friends and family will appreciate your new skills.

Fishing

The Italians love to fish. The country is surrounded by water and also boasts numerous lakes and streams. Grab a fishing rod, pack some cheese and bread, and partake in a tradition that is as old as the hills.

Bocce

Bocce traces its roots to the early Roman emperors, and Augustus is said to have been fond of this game. At one time, it became so addictive that people would play it instead of working. Venice officially outlawed bocce in 1576 because it had become such a bad habit for many. The law did little to stop the game's popularity.

Bocce is easy to learn, but hard to master. Studies have even shown that it helps with arthritis and other conditions, by providing exercise for the hand and wrist.

Wine

Wine can be found at almost every Italian meal. While the Italians did enjoy fine wines for special occasions, they also saw the value in local wine for their everyday consumption. It was very common for an Italian household to grow grapes or fruits in their back yard, to make wine from each fall. For many families, the wine recipes were passed down from generation to generation, improved on with each year's harvest.

Many wine shops now sell wine kits, which include all the equipment you need as well as starter grapes. Give a wine kit a try, and see how easy it is to make your own wine. Once you have the basic technique down, move on to making wine from your back yard apples, peaches, pears, plums and other fruits.

Italian Names and their Meanings

Is there a new child coming into your life? Or, possibly a pet, or even a boat or plane? Here are some traditional Italian names for you to consider to bring luck and good fortune.

Adrian / Adrianne: a city in Northern Italy
Angelo: angel
Anna: gracious
Antony: worthy of praise
Aria: melodious
Beatrice: blessed
Benedict: blessed
Camellia: an evergreen tree
Carina: darling
Carmela: garden
Concetta: pure
Donna: lady
Ezio: eagle
Fabrizio: craftsman
Francesca: free
Gabriela: devoted to God
Gemma: jewel
Giovanna: Italian form of "Jane"
Leonardo: strong as a lion Lorenzo: light
Maria: from Mary, the mother of Jesus
Marinna: from the sea
Pia: devout
Rosa: from the rose
Serena: serene, peaceful
Silvio: forest
Zaira: princess

The Italian Costume

Italians have always loved high fashion and sumptuous fabrics, and their clothing over the years has reflected this. From ancient Roman uniforms to medieval fineries through the incredible outfits of the Renaissance to the modern model runways, the Italians have led the way in stylish wear.

Here is a traditional outfit worn in the 1500s:

Italian Movies

Italian movies are often rich with emotion and commitment. When watching these movies, make sure to bring a tissue – you're sure to laugh or cry. Pour yourself some prosecco, put together a plate of cheese and fruit, and enjoy.

AMARCORD
In Italian with subtitles, this tale of Italy in the 1930s shows how traditional village life strives to continue despite the growing fascism of the government.

ATTILA
This miniseries traces the fighting of Attila the Hun, who covets and works to conquer the Roman Empire. While not incredibly accurate, it's still an enjoyable romp through a very bloody stage in Roman history.

BARRABAS
Anthony Quinn stars in this 1961 epic about the Roman Empire and death of Christ. Scenes of the Roman gladiator battles feature elephants, lions, and chariots.

BEN HUR
The classic chariot race is just one part of this movie set during the Roman Empire. Charlton Heston and Stephen Boyd star as friends who are pulled apart as they grow older. The epic won 11 Oscars.

THE BICYCLE THIEF
This sad tale shows how severely the depression after World War II affected most Italians. A father finally finds a job as a poster-hanger, and his wife sells their sheets to get him an old bicycle. On his very first day at work his bike is stolen, and he and his son search all over Rome to try to find the bike, so they do not starve.

BREAD AND CHOCOLATE
An Italian man goes off to Switzerland, leaving behind his family

and promising to return to them when he has enough money. He becomes fond of his new situation and even though he loses his work permit, he finds other ways to stay.

BREAD AND TULIPS
Winner of many awards, Silvio Soldini directs this tale of a middle-aged housewife who hitchhikes to Venice to find new joy in life.

CLEOPATRA
The 1963 classic starting Elizabeth Taylor and Richard Burton shows how the young, intelligent Egyptian queen captured the love of Julius Caesar and Marc Anthony. Cleopatra was described by her contemporaries as "well versed in the natural sciences and mathematics. She speaks seven languages proficiently. Were she not a woman one would consider her to be an intellectual." Note that the lead actor and actress were falling in love with one another during the filming!

CALIGULA
Definitely a movie for adults only, with a lot of explicit sex and violence. A cautionary tale of how much power can corrupt, as it drives Caligula to feel he can do whatever he wishes sexually and physically to others. Gorgeous costumes and Italian landscapes.

CITY OF WOMEN
Fellini's exploration of the feminist movement doesn't really have a plot, but is more a collection of stories about the different ways in which women think about themselves.

DEMETRIUS AND THE GLADIATORS
This movie was the sequel to The Robe. It tells of Demetrius, the Greek slave, who tries to protect the robe of Christ from the grasp of Caligula. He is tricked into believing his true love is dead, and turns to a life as a gladiator.

DIVORCE, ITALIAN STYLE
First released in the 1960's, Divorce, Italian Style is in Italian with English subtitles. This comedy is well rated by most reviewers. Marcello Mastroianni is a rich Sicilian lord who becomes bored

with his life. He wants a change and decides his wife must go. He becomes infatuated with his cousin, but divorce is illegal. He therefore tries to frame his wife with a lover so that he can kill her out of jealousy.

8 1/2
This classic from the 1960's is still powerful today. Marcello Mastroianni plays Guido, a filmmaker who is very popular but who becomes unsure of his work.

THE FALL OF THE ROMAN EMPIRE
This epic has numerous stories and stars filling it out. Alec Guinness, Christopher Plummer, Sophia Loren, Omar Sharif, James Mason and many others carry the story along. The landscapes are gorgeous and the costumes and scenery are quite impressive.

A FISTFUL OF DOLLARS
This classic "spaghetti western" was based on the classic Yojimbo by Akira Kurosawa, and starred Clint Eastwood. Shot in Italy by Sergio Leone, it became a huge hit and spawned two more movies in this series. It was then dubbed into English and enjoyed by American audiences. It tells a tale of a lone gunman who sets rival clans against each other.

FOR A FEW DOLLARS MORE
The second of the spaghetti western series by Sergio Leone, this film featured Clint Eastwood along with Lee Van Cleef, who came out of retirement to perform. This film breathed new life into their careers.

GLADIATOR
This movie was best viewed on the big screen, because of its sweeping landscapes and larger-than-life battles. The soundtrack is incredible, and the cinematography is lush. The characters are completely believable and compelling. Highly recommended.

GODFATHER 1
The classic Italian movie featuring a cavalcade of stars. Many of the scenes were shot in Sicily, and the wedding scene done in Sicily is extremely authentic. Classic quote: "In Sicily, women are more

dangerous than shotguns."

GODFATHER 2
The story continues, and there are even more great scenes filmed in Sicily. You can see the young Vito smuggled out on a donkeypast some village buildings in Sicily that you can still go and visit today.

GODFATHER 3
The finale to the saga, with very mixed reviews. Al Pacino tries to pass the family along to Andy Garcia and make amends for the things he's done in his life.

THE GOOD, THE BAD AND THE UGLY
The final movie in the spaghetti western trilogy by Sergio Leone, this film brings back Clint Eastwood and Lee Van Cleef along with newcomer Eli Wallach.

I, CLAUDIUS
Derek Jacobi stars as Claudius in this well received miniseries. George Baker is Tiberius, his son, and John Hurt is Caligula. A rich story of the plots and schemes of the Roman Empire.

IT STARTED IN NAPLES
Clark Gable and Sophia Loren star in this romance set in Naples. If you're able to visit this area of Italy, you'll find that many of the locations visited are still there. Lovely landscapes and costumes.

JULIET OF THE SPIRITS
Juliet is a middle-aged woman who loves her husband, but as she grows and matures through the movie, she is able to cope with his infidelity and find new strength.

JULIUS CAESAR
In the 1970's version, Charlton Heston plays Marc Anthony and John Gielgud plays Caesar. The Heston speech over the dead body of Caesar is especially noteworthy.

LADYHAWKE

This story is based on a medieval traditional love story. The man and woman are cursed, so that during the day she is a hawk and at night he is a wolf. The only time they can be together is during the brief moments of sunrise and sunset, when both are changing forms. This is filmed at three castles in northern Italy, and in the surrounding landscapes.

LIFE IS BEAUTIFUL
A movie which is both comedic and tragic. A young Jewish boy, Guido, in fascist Italy marries his childhood sweetheart and raises a son—but they are soon thrown into a concentration camp. Guido invents elaborate stories to help shield his son from the horrors going on around them. Roberto Benigni, who played Guido, won an Oscar for his performance.

MALENA
The very powerful story of a small town during World War II in Italy. Malena is a beautiful woman whose husband is off fighting in the war. Renato is a twelve year old boy who becomes infatuated with her. When Malena's husband is killed, the town becomes very hostile towards her, suspicious of her beauty to the point where they try to starve her to death.

THE MERCHANT OF VENICE
Lawrence Olivier shines as Shylock in the 1973 telling of the classic Shakespearian story. Some complain that this movie version emphasizes the tragic parts of the tale, ignoring the comedic elements.

MUCH ADO ABOUT NOTHING
Shakespeare's words are just as thrilling today as they were centuries ago, and the pairing of Kenneth Branagh and Emma Thompson is a treat to watch. A glorious romp through an Italian manor, with streaming sunshine and grapes on the vine. A lot of confusion and bother, and an ending full of love.

THE MONSTER
A con man is thought to be a notorious killer, and the police try to entrap him. Love, romance and great comedy results!

NAME OF THE ROSE
One of my favorite movies of all time. Sean Connery is brilliant in this adaptation of the Umberto Eco book. He's a monk that enjoys using his reason to solve puzzles, and who values the priceless treasure of books.

ORLANDO
A gorgeous adaptation of the famous novel by Virginia Woolf. The original story was apparently created when Virginia heard of a famous Italian noblewoman, intelligent and smart, who could not inherit her property because she was female. In the book and movie, Orlando is a male who is commanded by Queen Elizabeth never to age. At some point in the story "he" becomes "she" and although "she" is exactly the same person, she now cannot own the land because of her gender.

OTHELLO
Shakespeare's story of betrayal stars Lawrence Fishburne and Kenneth Branagh. Othello is a Moorish general who is very insecure in his love for his wife, Desdemona. Iago, played by Branagh, deliberately deceives Othello into believing his love is untrue, and Othello kills her for her suspected betrayal.

IL POSTINO
A small fishing village in Italy is the setting for this story. A shy postman becomes friends with a Cuban poet, and learns to think about his village in poetic terms, and to become more lyrical himself in his talks with his neighbors.

QUO VADIS?
Robert Taylor and Deborah Kerr star in this story of love during the Roman Empire. Taylor is a soldier who falls for Lygia, a slave girl. Emperor Nero is slowly going crazy, and the Christians are being persecuted.

THE ROBE
This movie stars Richard Burton as Marcellus Gallio. Gallio wins the robe of Jesus during a gambling game, and then feels he is under a curse for having it. His servant has at this point taken it to the

Middle East, and Gallio sets out to get it back to destroy it. Along the way, he converts and gains faith. The sequel to this was Demetrius and the Gladiators.

ROMAN HOLIDAY
Starring Gregory Peck and Audrey Hepburn, this movie brought fame and fortune to Hepburn. She is an European princess who wants to see the 'real world' of Rome, and finds a newspaper reporter (Peck) to help her out. Hepburn won an Oscar for her portrayal, and her gorgeous outfits won a costume design Oscar.

ROME ADVENTURE
This 1960's love story features a young schoolteacher who decides to go to Italy to find love. She first becomes fond of an artist, but when the artist's ex-girlfriend shows up, she turns to an older man.

ROME – POWER AND GLORY
This 5 hour documentary covers the rise and fall of the Roman empire, discussing the home life, political change, religious atmosphere, and leisure time of the Romans. A great introduction to the subject.

ROMEO AND JULIET
Probably the best known version of this play is the Franco Zeffirelli version released in 1968, which casts teenagers in the title roles. Michael York plays Tybalt, and you get easily drawn into the fierce passion and love which is often part of young first love.

ROOM WITH A VIEW
The tale of a young English girl who is being raised to do the Right Thing, and who falls in love with a boy in Italy on vacation. In the end, she ends up doing what will make her truly happy.

THE SEDUCTION OF MIMI
A fun comedy of interwoven sex lives. A man leaves his wife and falls in love with another woman, having a child with her. His wife, feeling neglected, takes up with another man.

SEEKING ASYLUM

This fun comedy film involves a kindergarten teacher who takes an unorthodox approach to learning.

SUMMERTIME
Katherine Hepburn stars in this romantic tale set in Venice. The movie features gorgeous views of Venice, its buildings, canals, and landscapes.

SPARTACUS
Starring Kirk Douglas, Spartacus is a 1960's movie which tells of a slave's rebellion against his Roman masters. This star-studded epic features Peter Ustinov, Anthony Hopkins, Tony Curtis, Jean Simmons, and Laurence Olivier.

TAMING OF THE SHREW
Elizabeth Taylor and Richard Burton pair up with Franco Zeffirelli for this adaptation of the Shakespeare classic. The Italian tradition of 'the oldest daughter must marry first' holds firm in this movie, and the gentle younger sister, Bianca (Natasha Pyne) has to wait until her older sister Katrina (Liz Taylor) finds a husband before she can be wed. Unfortunately, it is a challenge to find anyone willing to partner up with Katrina.

THREE COINS IN THE FOUNTAIN
Three American women each wish for love and romance in Rome. Each has a different type of romance. The beautiful Italian setting won the movie an Oscar for cinematography.

TITUS
Many dislike this Shakespeare play for its gore, but Anthony Hopkins does a good job with this 2000 release. It brings in modern references to show that mindless revenge and violence is not something of the past, it's with humanity at every stage of our evolution.

VARIETY LIGHTS
Fellini directs this classic show business story of an older stage manager who falls for a young, sexy starlet and helps to promote her to fame and fortune.

Visiting Italy

Tell me with whom you go and I'll tell you what you are.

—Italian proverb

If you're 18 or 80, dating or celebrating your 50th wedding anniversary, Italy is a land of love and romance. Take a trip there, visit the canals of Venice or the streets of Rome, and step back in time to a land of roses and wine!

Venice

Venice is one of the most romantic towns in the world. This classic Italian location actually consists of 120 separate islands, with 177 canals between them, and 450 bridges. There aren't any cars here— just walkways, gondolas, and other boats. Perfect for a strolling adventure at your own pace!

At the center of Venice is the Grand Canal. This gorgeous waterway is a great place to see by gondola, with red-and-white striped moorings lining the sides of the waterway. There are many shops and restaurants alongside.

Another place to visit is the Campanile de San Marco. It's a 10th century church, and you can climb all the way to the top of the structure to get a beautiful view of the city. Be sure to stop by Saint Mark's Square to have a cup of coffee and watch the passers-by.

Nearby Verona is the land of Romeo and Juliet. There is a balcony which is claimed to belong to the woman who inspired the tale, and a statue of her has been polished by being rubbed by people hoping for luck in love.

Rome

Rome is a city that has stood for centuries, and whose history still catches our imagination. Rome was the hub of a massive empire and the center of education and learning for centuries. The architecture and sights here could easily take many months to view.

One of the highlights is the Sistine Chapel, with its famous paintings. St Peter's Basilica is another must-see spot on any tour.

For the lovers of ancient culture, go through the Coliseum and Pantheon, and marvel at how these great buildings were created in a time before modern machinery.

For those who want to shop or eat, the restaurants and stores in Rome are an amazing combination of old style Italian and new style modern. You can find anything you want here, from Korean and Russian food to the most scrumptious native dishes.

Tuscany

Tuscany has a simply beautiful landscape with twisting rivers, quiet mountains, and sun-drenched beaches. Its beauty has inspired many poets, artists and writers to new heights. In addition to its many natural treasures, this area also boasts the Chianti wine region, which produces some of Italy's finest wines. Chianti is a fruity red wine which goes perfectly with many styles of Italian cuisine.

Towns to visit in this region include Florence, Lucca, Arezzo and Cortona. Florence was a center of learning and artistry during the

Renaissance, and was ruled by the Medici family. World-famous artists such as Botticelli and Donatello worked here. There are literally hundreds of historic buildings, locations, and artworks in Florence, including the Piazza del Duomo and Piazza della Signoria.

The Chianti wineries welcome visitors and provide tours and tastings. Call ahead to the various wineries of the Chianti region to find out their hours, and swing by for some tastings!

Be sure to visit Tuscany in the spring or fall. It can become extremely hot during the summer, and winter can be very brisk.

Sicily

Sicily boasts many cultures on a small island network. Its location in the center of the Mediterranean ensures it has not only Italian but also Greek and African influences. The Romans used it as their granary, the Arabs as a convenient docking spot on their voyages.

Sicily's food is world famous, drawing from its many cultures. Pasta is at the core of its various recipes, and seafood also figures prominently. Sicilian capers are famous around the world for their flavor.

Sicily's wine export—Marsala—is a rich drink that provides a delicious flavor to cooking as well. The wine is the perfect pairing to Sicilian desserts of pistachios, almonds, and honey dishes.

Sicily is not just one island, but many. Lipari is the largest of the islands and has a number of museums as well as a castle and cathedral. Salina is the second largest, and is famous for its fishing. Panarea is known for its scuba diving and fine restaurants.

Pisa

One of the most famous buildings in the world is the Leaning Tower of Pisa. This tower was built as a bell tower for the Pisa Cathedral. Construction began in 1173. It is unknown who the original architect was, and construction continued for over 200 years.

The tower was originally designed to be straight, but began leaning even during the building process. Construction was halted many times while the builders worked to try to fix the leaning, and replacing columns that had cracked under the strain of the slant. In the end, the tower could only be stabilized at a certain angle.

Pisa is also well known for its many museums and art galleries. The best time of year to visit Pisa is on June 16th, which is the day of the Luminara of Saint Ranieri. On this day, over seventy thousand candles are lit along the banks of the Arno River. The candles are set up to highlight the windows and outlines of the buildings along the banks. This has been done for special occasions since the early 1600s, but became an annual tradition in 1688 during a feast for Saint Ranieri.

Vatican City

For over a thousand years, the Pope in Italy held control of provinces directly. In the late 1800s, as Italy moved towards a republic state, the holdings of the Pope became fewer and fewer. In 1929, a special area, named Vatican City, was set aside for the Pope and became completely independent from Italian law and rule.

Vatican City is wholly enclosed by the city of Rome. It is only .44 square kilometers, which is about ¾ the size of the Mall in Washington DC. About 900 people live within this area. It is guarded by the Swiss Papal Guards and derives its income through donations and sales of its books and holy items.

Vatican City boasts several museums and priceless works of art. Perhaps the best known artwork is the Sistine Chapel, created by Michelangelo in the late 1400s and recently restored to its original brilliance. The frescoes portray stories from the lives of Moses and Christ.

The Pope does hold special masses – check ahead of time to see what special events and festivals would be going on during your visit.

Glossary of Italian Terms

baciami: kiss me bellissima: beautiful

bomboniera: sugar-coated almonds gathered in tulle fabric, used as wedding favors. The bags should always contain an odd number of almonds.

la borsa:A satin bag carried by the bride, to collect wedding money in during the reception.

buste: The tradition of the bride gathering money during a wedding.

cappuccino: a pressurized form of coffee which is made individually for each drinker.

confetti: candy-covered almonds, a traditional treat at weddings. famiglia: family

fiore: flower

I love you: ti amo

impalmamento: the handshake between the two fathers which would initiate a wedding arrangement.

l'amico: friend love: amore

mal'occhio: The "evil eye", a curse. Many traditions surrounding Italian weddings are trying to protect the new couple from bad luck, or the "evil eye".

masciata: A message sent by a matchmaker, informing the father of the bride of an interested party.

matrimonium: The civil part of the wedding process, where land and other goods would be exchanged.

millefiore: A style of glassware which involves thousands of small glass 'flowers' pressed together to form a vase or other item.

regerre il moccolo: being frustrated by inactivity. sensale: matchmaker

sposalizio: the wedding ceremony.

tarantella: a spider-like dance done at weddings.

tocca ferro: a piece of iron carried by the groom to ward off the evil eye.

wanda: twisted, fried dough, traditionally served at wedding ceremonies

will you marry me?: Mi vuoi sposare?

Web Resources

General

http://mp_pollett.tripod.com/section6.htm

Andrea Pollett offers a variety of translated Italian poems.

http://www.virtualitalia.com/

Information on all aspects of Italian culture, from genealogy to travel, wine and more.

http://www.romanceclass.com

This site has everything romance-related, including an area on Italian love and romance!

Travel

http://www.italiantourism.com/

Massive tourism website contains information on cities, hotels, wine regions, holidays, spas, and more.

http://www.goitaly.com

Gorgeous photos and travel details help bring this site to life.

http://www.initaly.com/

Laid out by region, you can find great deals on B&Bs here as well as information about the region you choose to explore.

http://www.vatican.va

The official website of the Vatican City, home of the Pope.

http://www.knowital.com/

Information on hotels and lodging in Italy, plus maps and more.

Food

http://italianfood.bellaonline.com

Spice up your love life with these delicious recipes.

Dedication

This book is dedicated to my mother, Ann Waller. She has long been a fan of Italian culture, literature and music. She even volunteered to be an extra in a full performance of Aida when it was produced in her area. She married an Italian man and enjoys their many visits to the country of his ancestry.

Ann took me on a trip through Italy when I was a teenager. The visit opened my eyes to the many beautiful buildings, foods, and wines that the country has to offer. Later in life, she took me on a two-week cruise around Italy. It was stunning. Thanks to her, I now seek out Italian delicacies, enjoy Italian wines, and appreciate all that the Italian culture has brought to the world.

I wish to thank these individuals who made Weddings and Courtships: France possible:

Jody Zolli, Jenn Mottram, Maureen O'Brien, Shirley Starke, Bob See, and Debi Gardiner.

About the Author

Lisa Shea is enamored with the classic beauty of Italy. From the canals of Venice to the majesty of Rome, from the vineyards of Tuscany to the coastlines of Sicily, there are stunning landscapes to be found in every direction.

There are countless types of delicious wine, a plethora of food options, plus music, dancing, friendship and joy in every town and village of this wonderful country. The peaceful bliss of a gondola ride is something that every couple should experience at least once.

Lisa has been writing about romance since her school days, and it was inevitable that one of her first books on romantic traditions focuses on the beautiful romantic splendor of Italy.

The Wedding & Courtships series:

Weddings & Courtships: Ireland

http://www.weddingsandcourtships.com/ireland/

Weddings & Courtships: France

http://www.weddingsandcourtships.com/france/

Weddings & Courtships: Italy

http://www.weddingsandcourtships.com/italy/

Medieval romance novels:
Knowing Yourself
Seeking the Truth
Finding Peace
A Sense of Duty
Creating Memories
Looking Back
Badge of Honor
Lady in Red
Believing your Eyes
Trusting in Faith
Sworn Loyalty
In A Glance

Cozy romance murder mystery series:
Aspen Allegations | Birch Blackguards | Cedar Conundrums

Blackstone Valley mystery novelette series:
Rumble Strip

Sci-fi adventure romance series:
Aquarian Awakenings | Betelgeuse Beguiling | Centauri Chaos |
Draconis Discord

Dystopian journey series:
Into the Wasteland | He Who Was Living | Broken Images

Scottish regency time-travel series:
One Scottish Lass | A Time Apart | A Circle in Time

1800s Tennessee black / Native American series:
Across the River | In the Pines

Sci-fi and Massachusetts short stories:
Chartreuse | The Angst of Change | BAAC | Melting | Armsby

Black Cat short stories:
The Lucky Cat – Black Cat Vol. 1

Here are a few of Lisa's self-help books:

Yoga for Stress Relief and Forgiveness
Step by step guidance to improving your health and serenity

Journaling Basics – Journal Writing for Beginners
Everything you need to know to get started with journaling

Quick No-Cook Low Carb Recipes
Heathy, easy recipes with low sugar

Secrets to Falling Asleep
Get better sleep to improve health and reduce stress

Dream Symbol Encyclopedia
Interpretation and meaning of dream symbols

Lucid Dreaming Guide
Foster creativity in a lucid dream state

Learning to say NO – and YES! To your Dream
Protect your goals while gently helping others succeed

Reduce Stress Instantly
Practical relaxation tips you can use right now for instant stress relief

Time Management Course
Learn to end procrastination, increase productivity, and reduce stress

Simple Ways to Make the World Better for Everyone
Every day we wake up is a day to take a fresh path, to help a friend, and to improve our lives.

"Be the change you wish to see in the world."